Dream in Progress

by

Kathleen Emerson Stulce

© 2017

Published in the United States by Nurturing Faith Inc., Macon GA,

www.nurturingfaith.net.

Library of Congress Cataloging-in-Publication Data is available.

ISBN 978-1-63528-007-4

All rights reserved. Printed in the United States of America.

Scripture quotations are from New Revised Standard Version Bible: Catholic Edition, copyright © 1989, 1993 National Council of the Churches of Christ in the United States of America. Used by permission. All rights reserved worldwide.

Scripture taken from the Common English Bible®, CEB® Copyright © 2010, 2011 by Common English Bible.™ Used by permission. All rights reserved worldwide.

Image page 76 by Amid The World, lightstock_366465, https://www.lightstock.com/photos/elderly-man-praying-over-a-bible

Image page 82 by skeeze, https://pixabay.com/en/silhouettes-people-worker-dusk-582969/

Image page 89 by Bavali Yan, https://stocksnap.io/photo/GAS5UZWDUD

Image page 97 by Alex Kriver, https://www.pexels.com/photo/man-mountain-sports-activity-26851/

Image page 107 by Frank McKenna, https://stocksnap.io/photo/DXRGHFDOI3

Dedication

I dedicate this to my parents,
Charles Emerson and Betty Mae Jordan Emerson,
who grounded me in these biblical stories and prepared the soil
from which my faith would grow and flourish.

A Dream in Progress offers familiar Bible stories in bite-sized portions that are thought-provoking and spiritually satisfying. Readers can anticipate faithful and creative commentary followed by questions and pauses that prompt personal reflection and prayer. Keep your journal and pen ready as you—along with Joseph, Samuel, Daniel and Jonah—receive messages from God!

Mary Jayne Allen
Minister of Education (ret.), First Baptist Church, Chattanooga, Tennessee

From her wealth of experience as a social worker, spiritual director and pastor, Kate Stulce brings a refreshing book of meditation offerings that challenges us all to follow our dreams. With substantial biblical knowledge, Kate encourages her readers with words that are applicable and practical, yet moving and motivating. Readers will appreciate the creative, visionary insights that reflect Kate's own search for authentic and deeply meaningful relationship with the spirit of God as well as her desire to encourage others on their journeys.

Rev. Leslie Etheredge,
Western Regional Minister, Florida Conference, United Church of Christ

It's a common refrain in our culture today: follow your dreams! Many people are probably surprised to learn that this is also an admonishment from the Bible. Throughout the sacred text, prophets and leaders are inspired by dreams to follow a path where the Spirit of God is leading.

The Rev. Kathleen Stulce reflects with her readers on biblical images that invite us to follow our dreams. In gentle writing that at times takes on a poetic rhythm, she invites readers to discover Divine Inspiration of their own dreams. As a spiritual director and social worker, Kate brings to life biblical images and metaphors making them relevant and accessible for today. This series of meditations is sure to enliven and inspire those with the wisdom to sit with these meditations and allow them to take root in their lives.

The Rev. Louis F. Kavar, Ph.D.
Author, *The Integrated Self: A Holistic Approach to Spirituality and Mental Health Practice*

Prologue

"Is it not known to all people that the dream is the most usual way of God's revelation to humankind?"
—Tertullian

"In a dream, in a vision of the night, when deep sleep falls upon mortals, when they slumber on their beds, then God opens their ears."
—Job 33:15-16

There are 700 references to dreams in the Bible. God was understood to speak through dreams and visions, connecting God to the people. Because dreams were so revered, interpretations were of the utmost importance. Kings made critical decisions based on such interpretations, influencing entire nations and the future of their people.

Dream in Progress is the product of my longtime fascination with dreams. Divided into three sections of meditations, each section or "book" is based on a different story in the Bible.

Book I, *OUR STORY BEGINS: God's Faithfulness Sustains in Human Tragedy*, comes from Genesis, detailing Joseph's dreams and their impact on his life and the lives of many others.

Book II, *OUR STORY EVOLVES: God's Spirit Prevails in Human Weakness*, is drawn from I Samuel where the young Samuel hears God's voice in the night and eventually leads the nation of Israel.

Book III, *OUR STORY CONTINUES: God's Truth Surfaces in Human Tales*, is taken from the books of Daniel and Jonah, where we follow the folktales of Daniel, another dream interpreter, contrasted with the parable of Jonah.

Scriptures quoted in Book I and Book II come from the New Revised Standard Version of the Bible, Catholic Edition, Anglicized Text. In Book III, the Common English Bible translation is utilized.

My hope is that these meditations will bring life to these familiar Bible stories and that you will discover application to your own life as you read them.

Many blessings as you do.

Contents

Prologue.. v

Our Story Begins 1

Our Story Evolves 43

Our Story Continues 75

Our Story Begins

God's Faithfulness Sustains in Human Tragedy

Dreams

Genesis 37:2-11

This is the story of the family of Jacob.
Joseph, being seventeen years old, was shepherding the flock with his brothers…'
And Joseph brought a bad report to their father. "Now Israel loved Joseph more than any other of his children, because he was the son of his old age; and he had made him a long robe with sleeves. But when his brothers saw that their father loved him more than all his brothers, they hated him, and could not speak peaceably to him. "Once Joseph had a dream, and when he told it to his brothers, they hated him even more. He said to them, 'Listen to this dream that I dreamed. There we were, binding sheaves in the field. Suddenly my sheaf rose up and stood upright; then your sheaves gathered around it, and bowed down to my sheaf.' His brothers said to him 'Are you indeed to reign over us? Are you indeed to have dominion over us?' So they hated him even more because of his dreams and words.

Meditation 1

Dreams—Our "Personal Scriptures"

Seventeen…no longer a child…not yet an adult. Joseph lives in limbo. Long his father's clearly favored child, he even wears a special robe made for him by his father. The long sleeves indicate his special status. Workers wear short sleeves but Joseph is not a worker in the conventional sense. His elevated relationship with his father seems to put him in a role as monitor of his older brothers. He "brings reports" to his father. Perhaps these are embellished a bit for effect, as Joseph is a dreamer and a storyteller. It is easy to imagine him filling his time designing seemingly impossible plots to escape this dreary life. How could he, who so obviously has received the message that he is special, above ordinary tasks, be expected to work with his brothers in the fields? "Surely I am destined for greater things," Joseph must tell himself.

And then he has a dream.

In his dream, he is working the fields with his brothers and his sheaf of grain suddenly stands upright and all their sheaves bow down to his.

Being seventeen, he is sometimes inclined to be a little impulsive, a little cocky, and even a little arrogant. That might be forgiven except for Joseph's brothers' long history of Jacob's preference for Joseph and Joseph's willingness to flaunt his favored position.

Joseph, not mature enough to ponder the dream, offer it to God for God to bless its meaning, sees this as a sign: yes, indeed, his day is coming, his path to greatness is unfolding. Perhaps in his excitement he blurts it out. Maybe out of habit he assumes a superior posture. Maybe he experiences this as an opportunity to exact some kind of revenge for hurts they have inflicted on him. Whatever his motives, his actions set in motion the vengeance that later will be carried out by his brothers.

Sacred Ponderings
What dreams for my life do I have? Have I ever offered them to God for blessing?

Prayerful Pause
O, God, giver of dreams, giver of life, I pray for grace never to dismiss or misuse the dreams you give me. May I always be guided by your love as I seek to live them out.

Meditation 2

"We are made of dreams and bones"
—Appalachian folk song

If we imagine that Joseph's dreams are disregarded as foolishness we seriously underestimate the regard given dreams by the Hebrews, who believe that dreams are connections to God. They know that kings' dreams can serve as the basis for major decisions and can influence a country's going to war or in other ways affect the people's wellbeing and future.

Were dreams held in less esteem by the culture, Joseph's siblings might be slightly more inclined to ignore him. Instead, his report of his dream only fuels the flame of long established sibling rivalry.

Jacob himself was involved in such a conflict with his brother Esau, Jacob having been the favored child of Rebecca. The "tradition" then continued, with Jacob being tricked by Laban to marry Leah, when Jacob truly loved and wanted to marry Leah's sister Rachel. Jacob ultimately worked 14 years before he earned Rachel, his preferred bride, to be his wife. As if that were not enough to create dissension, Leah began to bear son after son, while Rachel remained barren, a terrible curse in their culture. When Rachel finally gives birth to Joseph, the stage is set for the rivalry between Joseph and his half-brothers.

Sacred Ponderings
What family heritage affects my hopes, my dreams, my thoughts, and my behavior? Do I carry any emotional scars from that history? If so, am I willing to examine them in the light of God's grace?

Prayerful Pause
God of grace, may I trust you to weave a beautiful tapestry from all the threads of my life.

Meditation 3

*"Faith is the assurance of things hoped for,
the conviction of things not seen."*
Hebrews 11:1

What intense anger is seething and growing within Joseph's siblings every passing year, as they witness their father's pampering of Joseph. And Joseph, enjoying this spotlight, relishes telling them his dreams., But when he reports dreaming that the sun and moon and eleven stars bowed to him, even Jacob, the doting father, rebukes him—small comfort to his other sons.

However, for some time Jacob has not exerted much positive influence on his family. His wives bicker. His children are full of resentment. The sons of Leah, Jacob's first wife, trick and murder an entire community of men in their fury over their sister Dinah's impregnation by Shechem. This is despite Shechem's apparent love for Dinah and his arrangement with Jacob to marry her. This tragedy spurs Jacob to make efforts to reestablish his relationship with God and to direct his family to purify themselves, to put away any relics of worship of foreign gods, and to lead them on a holy pilgrimage to Bethel.

So when Joseph shares his dreams, Jacob ponders this within himself. Perhaps some bit of hope stirs in him that Joseph, this son whom he so dearly loves, whose immaturity sometimes masks his promise of greatness, will be used of God in a way as yet to be revealed.

Having been reminded by God on his pilgrimage to Bethel that he was still the heir of the promises made to Abraham, Jacob begins to imagine a future for Joseph he has not allowed himself to consider for a great while.

Sacred Ponderings
With whom do I most identify in this story? What lessons are here for me about anger and bitterness?

Prayerful Pause
God, may I let go of any anger and resentment and allow your grace to pave the way to a more hopeful and peaceful future.

Disappointment

Genesis 37:12-35

"Then his brothers went to pasture their father's flock in Shechem. And Jacob said to Joseph, 'Are not your brothers pasturing the flock in Shechem? Come, and I will send you to them.' And he said, 'I will go.'

"…When they saw him from a distance and before he came close to them, they plotted against him."

Meditation 4

"Then the Lord said to Cain, 'Why are you angry? And why has your countenance fallen? If you do well, will not your countenance be lifted up? And if you do not do well, sin is crouching at the door; and its desire is for you, but you must master it."
Genesis 4:6-7

Perhaps for the livelihood of the sheep, perhaps to cool things down a bit, Jacob sends his older sons to pasture the flock. He is grieved by the alienation amongst his children. Does he instruct Joseph to apologize or merely send a restless teen on a task? Whatever, it is an unwitting error on Jacob's part.

Joseph's brothers see him coming in the distance. They have complained amongst themselves many times. Perhaps they have conspired a time or two (at least) to do him harm. Reuben, as the eldest son, has always prevailed against such plans. Joseph's bragging about his dream tips the balance. They agree to kill him. Reuben believes he has swayed them to give up this plot. He insists they put Joseph in a pit, secretly planning to return and free him once the others have calmed down. Reuben leaves, perhaps to tend a sheep or to get some distance from his ill-tempered brothers for a while.

Still stewing in their anger, the brothers are not about to be mollified by Reuben's efforts. When they see Ishmaelite traders, they flag them down and offer them a "slave." Now they are not only rid of him, they have made a profit as well! Twenty shekels of silver later and Joseph is on the road to Egypt.

Imagine Joseph trying to convince his new "owners" that those are his brothers, that this is a huge mistake. When he realizes there is no turning back, he is initially angry. How could they do this to him? And then he thinks of the arrogant things he has said, his disregard for their feelings. He thinks of his father's certain distress when he doesn't return with his brothers. He misses his father. He even begins to miss his brothers. He wishes he could return home and apologize. His heart is full of regret.

Sacred Ponderings
When have I acted too hastily, as Joseph's brothers? When have I been thoughtless of others, as Joseph? What actions have left me filled with regret?

Prayerful Pause
God, draw my awareness to those behaviors that need changing and give me courage to deal with them. Cleanse me of regrets and fill me with gratitude for a fresh beginning.

Meditation 5

"If grief is part of death, guilt is its twin."
—Betty Mae Jordan Emerson

If Joseph is distraught, he is not alone. Reuben is beside himself when he returns to realize what has happened. He was the eldest. He should have known better, he berates himself, than to leave his brothers alone; should have realized that they might do something like this. How could he have been so irresponsible? How can they now admit to their father what they have done? If they thought it was hard to live with their father's favoritism for Joseph, how will they ever live with his grief?

They frantically concoct a plan: they will present their father with a piece of the cloth from Joseph's special robe, of which they had stripped him. They will dip it in animal's blood and tell Jacob that Joseph was killed by a wild animal.

The resentment that has always been directed towards Joseph, they now turn on each other. Whose stupid idea was it, they argue amongst themselves, to sell him to the Ishmaelites? We could have scared him into submission when he was in the pit, one says. Reuben angrily silences them. They return home sullen and subdued, dreading to face the consequences of their actions.

Sacred Ponderings
Never once do we have record that these siblings, these descendants of Abraham, turned to their faith in this situation. How differently this could have turned out if they had!

Prayerful Pause
Dear God, in the midst of trouble, may You be the rock on which I rely.

Meditation 6

"Incline thine ear to my cry! For my soul has had enough of troubles, and my life has drawn near to Sheol."
Psalm 88:21-23

    Jacob is devastated. He has lost the first child that his beloved Rachel bore to him. And he has lost the hope of Joseph carrying out God's promises for Israel. His family attempts to comfort him, but he will not be comforted. If he had the energy he would be angry with his sons. But he is too soul-weary for that. Mostly he blames himself for ever sending Joseph on such an errand.

    The days seem endless to him. He has no interest in carrying on. Reuben takes on the task of keeping some semblance of order to their sheep-herding existence. His brothers are more responsive to his leadership, as they live with the quite apparent deterioration of their father. Occasionally, Jacob thinks on God's promise to him. But it seems a distant, faded memory, a lost dream.

Sacred Ponderings
How do I handle grief, loss, the disappointment when a dream fades?

Prayerful Pause
Dear God, envelop my heart with your tenderness and love whenever I am grieving, forlorn, feeling hopeless and deserted.

Drama and Deceit

Genesis 37:36 & 39:1-20

"Meanwhile the Midianites had sold him in Egypt to Potiphar, one of Pharaoh's officials, the Captain of the guard....The Lord was with Joseph, and he became a successful man; he was in the house of his Egyptian master. His master saw that the Lord was with him, and that the Lord caused all that he did to prosper. So Joseph found favor in his sight and attended him; he made him overseer of his house and put him in charge of all that he had...

"Now Joseph was handsome and good-looking. And after a time his master's wife cast her eyes on Joseph and said, 'Lie with me.' But he refused... One day, however, when he went into the house to do his work, and while no one else was in the house, she caught hold of his garment, saying 'Lie with me!' But he left his garment in her hand, and fled and ran outside... she called out to the members of her household and said to them, 'See, my husband has brought among us a Hebrew to insult us! He came in to me to lie with me, and I cried out with a loud voice'... When his master heard the words that his wife spoke to him, saying 'This is the way your servant treated me', he became enraged. And Joseph's master took him and put him into prison...'"

Meditation 7

"The thrill of glory…"

Just when life has looked about as bleak as it could get, Joseph's talents are noticed and rewarded by Potiphar, the officer of Pharaoh. He is given increasing responsibility and truly wins the trust of the master. Joseph's behavior and demeanor impress Potiphar that the Lord is with him and that the Lord is causing all that he does to "prosper in his hands." We almost sense the relief, Joseph beginning to see that his future may well be redeemed. God must surely be in all this, bringing this to some conclusion, blessed of God.

Perhaps God's praise is continually on his lips, but there is no mention of this. Perhaps, as we are prone to do, when things are going well we become complacent to God's presence and blessing. Certainly, he is kept busy with his many new duties. He is apparently naïve about the havoc Potiphar's wife is capable of wreaking. Engrossed in his responsibilities, he underestimates the danger that threatens his newfound status and the possibilities it presents him for a better life.

Sacred Ponderings
When have I become so involved in some task or aspect of my life, that I have lost perspective, perhaps risked my own wellbeing or that of others?

Prayerful Pause
God, I pray to stay focused on you through good times and bad, and to practice gratitude whatever my circumstances.

Meditation 8

"The agony of deceit..."

Joseph perhaps doesn't take Potiphar's wife's initial approaches very seriously. Her behavior may well be common with the servants—teasing, cajoling, and taking some pleasure in having control over them. Perhaps some of those imprisoned had been accused of the very same thing. Joseph's response was a resounding "NO!" Given the trust he knows he has earned, he apparently feels quite safe that this will be the end of it. Joseph seems to present more of a challenge to Potiphar's wife. The more vociferously he refuses, the angrier she becomes. Likely she is accustomed to less resistance. The fact that her husband thinks so highly of him only makes him that much more appealing, more of a "prize" to win. His vehement rebuff is not to go without the harshest of punishment.

At her first opportunity she begins to yell "foul" and gets the ear of her husband, making sure that she makes the point "The Hebrew servant whom you have brought among us, came in to insult me." What defense can Joseph possibly present? He has the master's trust. He has access to his wife. She has possession of his cloak. Everything points to it's being truth. Potiphar apparently feels he has been played the fool. Whatever divine blessing he had believed Joseph endowed with is quickly forgotten in the heat of anger.

Once again, Joseph finds himself in prison. And while he had certainly earned the wrath of his brothers, this time, to add insult to injury, he has done nothing wrong. In fact he has done everything to act honorably towards his employer.

Sacred Ponderings
When have I been treated unfairly? How did I respond? Am I aware of having treated others unjustly? Have I made amends where possible?

Prayerful Pause
May I willingly turn over old hurts to You for healing. And where I have been the transgressor, give me the courage to seek forgiveness and restitution.

Meditation 9

"The humiliation of defeat"

What a meteoric fall! Imagine returning to the prison you expected never to inhabit again, the taunts from some of the prisoners still there: "Thought you were a big shot, did you? Well, you're no better than the rest of us!" Perhaps a few are sympathetic: "I know. Everything seemed fine and all of a sudden I found myself here too." But this must be the loneliest, most agonizing time Joseph has ever experienced. At least before, there had been some hope, some possibility. How can he ever earn that much trust again, have that much opportunity? What would his brothers think if they could see him now? "Well, Joseph, where is your striped coat now? Where's all that importance you were going to lord over us? You're in prison for raping your master's wife? Well, well, we may be lowly sheepherders but we are free to roam." And his father! What would his father think of him if he realized his son's circumstances and the accusations against him? He can hardly bear the thoughts of the disgrace to his family; all the hopes and dreams his father had for him, his father's broken heart broken further.

Sacred Ponderings

What "falls from grace" have I experienced, perhaps of my own making, or worse, due to false accusations? In times of disgrace, loss of trust, isolation from friends, family, what has given my life meaning? Where do I turn and with what spirit do I meet these circumstances?

Prayerful Pause

God, grant me the grace to always turn to You and to always seek meaningful ways to confront my difficulties.

Dreams Delivered

Genesis 39:21-40:8

"But the Lord was with Joseph and showed him steadfast love; he gave him favour in the sight of the chief jailer. The chief jailer committed to Joseph's care all the prisoners who were in the prison, and whatever was done there, he was the one who did it...

"Some time after this, the cupbearer of the king of Egypt and his baker offended their lord the king of Egypt. Pharaoh was angry with his two officers, the chief cupbearer and chief baker, and he put them in custody in the house of the captain of the guard, in the prison where Joseph was confined. The captain of the guard charged Joseph with them, and he waited on them; and they continued some time both in custody. One night they both dreamed—the cupbearer and the baker of the king of Egypt, who were confined to prison—each his own dream, and each dream with its own meaning..."

Meditation 10

"I wait for the Lord, my soul waits and in his word I hope."
Psalm 130:5

Joseph apparently doesn't spend a lot of time in self-pity. The child who had roamed the fields while his brothers worked seems to have developed a good bit of self-discipline. He has learned that concentrating on doing a good job and being respectful of those about him is good medicine for his soul, and tends to win him regard and responsibility. He must begin to recognize that God has been his steadfast companion throughout these troubling, tumultuous times. Perhaps he begins to pray with gratitude for what he is learning and for the things God is already working out in ways Joseph cannot begin to imagine.

Sacred Ponderings
Am I allowing self-pity to put obstacles in my path? Have I focused on gratitude lately?

Prayerful Pause
Dear God, I pray for a grateful, patient heart and the awareness of Your companionship throughout my lifelong journey.

Meditation 11

"Here is my servant whom I uphold, my chosen, in whom my soul delights; I have put my spirit upon him..."
Isaiah 42:1

Somehow, in the midst of the worst circumstances, once again, Joseph finds favor. The captain of the guard puts Joseph in charge of the cupbearer and the chief baker, who, unfortunately, also have earned the wrath of Pharaoh. (What have THEY done, one wonders? Are the angers of Pharaoh and Potiphar visited upon their subjects with some frequency?) The captain of the guard may well have been associated with Joseph during his previous imprisonment and been impressed then with his comportment. Perhaps the captain of the guard has some compassion for these men, essentially in the same boat, and has the wisdom to see that it might be healing both for Joseph in serving them and for them in being served by Joseph. The Bible reports that "they continued for some time in custody." One imagines there may be plenty of time for sharing their distress, their longings, and bits of their histories. Joseph is likely a good listener who becomes a trusted companion.

Sacred Ponderings
Am I overlooking opportunities when I might be a healing influence on others? Am I taking time to really listen to others when they take the risk to share of themselves?

Prayerful Pause
O God, help me to remain sensitive to the urgings of the Spirit when opportunities present themselves for me to be a healing force. May I be willing to respond when You direct me. Amen.

Meditation 12

"When there are prophets among you, I the Lord make myself known to them in visions; I speak to them in dreams."
Numbers 12:6

Perhaps sleep provides great escape from the loneliness, the discomfort, the humiliation of incarceration. One imagines these men look forward to some respite from the grind of the long days. But on one particular night, both the cupbearer and the baker have very puzzling dreams. They awake, disturbed, somewhat disoriented, irritable, withdrawn.

Joseph has grown more sensitive over time to the moods, nonverbal cues, and nuances of behavior around him. He likely gives them some time to fully wake up. As they are more alert, he prods gently, "Why are your faces downcast today?"

Believed to be direct messages from God, their dreams carry great weight. The cupbearer and the baker feel compelled to share their dreams but they also express much trepidation. There is no one available to interpret them, and this is crucial. They are the recipients of clearly important, but cryptic, messages. But there is no "cryptologist," no court wizard to unscramble these dreams.

Joseph accepts the responsibility for this task, "steps up to the plate." He makes clear that interpretations belong to God. But he offers himself as God's vessel, and asks to hear the dreams.

Sacred Ponderings
Do I listen for God's direction even in the ordinary events of life—a conversation, a magazine or newspaper article, a song…a dream?

Prayerful Pause
May I remain open to all the ways you choose to speak to me, O God, and sensitive to Your Spirit when others share with me their search for You.

Dreams Decoded

Genesis 40:9-23

"So the chief cupbearer told his dream to Joseph, and said to him, 'In my dream there was a vine before me, and on the vine there were three branches. As soon as it budded, its blossoms came out and the clusters ripened into grapes. Pharaoh's cup was in my hand; and I took the grapes and pressed them into Pharaoh's cup, and placed the cup in Pharaoh's hand.' Then Joseph said to him, 'This is its interpretation; the three branches are three days; within three days Pharaoh will lift up your head and restore you to your office; and you shall place Pharaoh's cup in his hand, just as you used to do when you were his cupbearer. But remember me when it is well with you; please do me the kindness to make mention of me to Pharaoh, and so get me out of this place....

"When the chief baker saw that the interpretation was favorable, he said to Joseph, 'I also had a dream…

On the third day, which was Pharaoh's birthday, he made a feast for all his servants, and lifted up the head of the chief cupbearer and the chief baker among his servants. He restored the chief cupbearer to his cupbearing, and he placed the cup in Pharaoh's hand; but the chief baker he hanged, just as Joseph had interpreted to them. Yet the chief cupbearer did not remember Joseph, but forgot him."

Meditation 13

"Who knows what God will say to me today or to you today or into the midst of what unlikely moment He will choose to say it?"
—Frederick Buechner

The cupbearer apparently is more eager to share his dream, perhaps sensing within himself that his dream holds some promise. And, indeed, Joseph interprets that "within three days Pharaoh will lift up your head and restore you to your office; and you shall place Pharaoh's cup in his hand just as you used to do as his cupbearer."

Imagine the joyful response the cupbearer has, practically dancing around the cell. He either totally misses Joseph's words "But remember me when it is well with you; please do me the kindness to mention me to Pharaoh" or he mindlessly promises that, of course, he will. But he is still too focused on this good news to pay much attention to Joseph's need for some recognition of this interpretation to Pharaoh.

Joseph may be feeling some hope himself from this interpretation. If only the cupbearer keeps some little fragment of memory alive of this favor Joseph has requested…

Sacred Ponderings
When have I been thoughtless/careless in relation to promises I have made?

Prayerful Pause
O God, call to my mind those tasks I have promised to fulfill. May I remember those who depend on me to honor my commitments.

Meditation 14

"Every moment is a holy moment and all of life is grace."
—Frederick Buechner

Meanwhile, the baker, while still feeling some reservation, yet also some weak hope that the cupbearer's dream portends some promise for his dream as well, shares his vision with Joseph. Joseph, who just made the most gratifying interpretation the cupbearer might have hoped for, now is called upon to deliver devastating news to the baker: "Within three days Pharaoh will lift up your head—from you! -and hang you on a pole; and the birds will eat the flesh from you."

The cupbearer still dazed from his happy report, momentarily grieves with his friend the baker. But the grim interpretation spreads a pall over the prison cell. We can imagine Joseph is stricken for the man. We don't know what comfort Joseph or the cupbearer offer or what the baker is willing to receive. Does he curl up in a fetal position in his cell awaiting his fate? Does he rail against God for this injustice towards himself? Does he withdraw to pray silently to escape this tragic end… or courage to face it?

Sacred Ponderings

Is it a holy moment when Joseph delivers this heartbreaking interpretation? Is grace present in this situation? It has been said that "It is not the circumstances in which we find ourselves but the spirit with which we meet them, which constitutes our comfort." How does this apply in this story? In the story of my life?

Prayerful Pause

O God, may I accept cupbearer-type news or baker-type messages with faith that You are with me in whatever circumstance I find myself and trust that You will see me through it.

Meditation 15

"What is seen in dreams is but a reflection, the likeness of a face looking at itself."
Sirach 34:3

The baker has three long, yet too brief, days to consider what lies ahead. These three days involve preparations that are going on for the Pharaoh's birthday. Perhaps the baker ponders how he has lived his life, recalls better times, grieves his mistakes, poor judgments he has made. He hears Joseph's words again and again. He is facing death and examining himself, his life; the opportunities he was given and made use of, the ones he threw away.

One can only hope he makes some peace with God. It is easy, though, to imagine that, given the Pharaoh's propensity for the unpredictable, the baker hopes against hope that some generous spirit will overtake the Pharaoh at his birthday party. Perhaps he will grant the baker his life and the return to his position. And yet…there is that dream and what it represents….a death foretold. Sure enough, as Joseph has predicted, the baker is put to death…and the cupbearer, who joyfully returns to his former status, quickly forgets his promise to remember Joseph to the Pharaoh.

Sacred Ponderings
Every day is an opportunity to examine ourselves and take corrective action where needed.

Prayerful Pause
Dear God, may I not wait for a crisis in my life—life-threatening illness, the death of a friend, family member, relationship; financial problems or some other tragic circumstance—to take the time and effort to examine my life and offer it to the light of Your grace.

Dreams Delayed

Genesis 41:1-45

"After two whole years, Pharaoh dreamed that he was standing by the Nile, and there came up out of the Nile seven sleek and fat cows, and they grazed in the reed grass. Then seven other cows, ugly and thin, came up out of the Nile after them, and stood by the other cows on the bank of the Nile. The ugly and thin cows ate up the seven sleek and fat cows. And Pharaoh awoke. Then he fell asleep and dreamed a second time; seven ears of grain, plump and good, were growing on one stalk. Then seven ears, thin and blighted by the east wind, sprouted after them. The thin ears swallowed up the seven plump and full ears. Pharaoh awoke, and it was a dream. In the morning his spirit was troubled; so he sent and called for all the magicians of Egypt and all its wise men.

Pharaoh told them his dreams, but there was no one who could interpret them to Pharaoh. "Then the chief cupbearer said to Pharaoh, 'I remember my faults today..."

Meditation 16

"In what time I am afraid, I will trust in thee."
Psalm 56:3

A few days pass…then a few weeks…the weeks turn into months…. Initially Joseph hopes that the cupbearer is just looking for the right moment to speak to the Pharaoh. He then considers that perhaps Potiphar is still so angry with Joseph that he influences Pharaoh to refuse to honor the request on Joseph's behalf. Or, what if, God forbid, that the cupbearer has suffered severe consequences for even asking? Joseph listens for news of the cupbearer. Sometimes he again plays through what else he might have done in response to Potiphar's wife. What might have avoided this outcome that keeps him imprisoned? He ponders if perhaps Potiphar's wife remains an obstacle to his release, adamant that Joseph must never be restored to his position. He clings to his faith, that somehow God is working in ways not yet apparent.

Finally, two years later, the Pharaoh has a fitful night of disturbing dreams… seven thin cows devour seven fat cows; seven blighted ears of grain consume seven healthy ears of grain. Certainly these dreams seem related and seem to foretell some ill fate. But what? Pharaoh is responsible for this country and his people. He must get to the bottom of this and avert whatever this disaster is that surely must be coming. He calls all the magicians of Egypt and all the wise men. But not a one of them are able to provide any interpretations. The anxiety level around the palace escalates. Is there no hope of unraveling this mystery? Meanwhile, Joseph hears rumors that the Pharaoh has had bad dreams. But no one has yet sought him out to decipher their meaning. He entreats God, "Does no one remember me? What can the future possibly hold if I don't get this opportunity?"

Sacred Ponderings
What do I do when I am puzzled, frightened, and fearful of the unknown?
How do I handle a fading sense of hope?

Prayerful Pause
God of hope, help me to stay calm and to think clearly in those times when I am prone to give in to anxiety and despair.

Meditation 17

"Look on my misery and rescue me, for I do not forget your law. Plead my cause and redeem me."
Psalm 119: 153-154

As the Pharaoh's growing frustration penetrates the palace, suddenly the cupbearer recalls his experience of sharing his dream with Joseph. Perhaps he is not keen to revisit that period of his life when he was imprisoned. But he feels a loyalty to Joseph. And he would gladly be the one to offer a workable solution to the beleaguered Pharaoh. He says to Pharaoh: "I remember my faults today." He shares the dream he had during his incarceration and the young Hebrew captain of the guard who accurately interpreted it.

One can only imagine Joseph's relief/excitement/uncertainty as he is rushed from his prison cell to clean up for presentation to the Pharaoh. Since the last time he has had contact with Pharaoh he has gone through the most humiliating experience of his life. Pharaoh would surely have heard all about that. But Joseph need not worry that there will be rehashing of the past. The Pharaoh gets right to the point: "I have had a dream, and there is no one who can interpret it. I have heard it said of you that when you hear a dream you can interpret it." Joseph quickly gives the credit to God and almost as quickly provides the meaning. Following seven productive years, famine will come and the doubling of the dream means that God is letting him know that these events will be unfolding soon.

Joseph recommends that the Pharaoh select someone to oversee the land to ensure that stores of food are set aside during the productive years. Thus, they can survive the famine that will inevitably come. One can almost hear the collective sigh throughout the palace.

Sacred Ponderings
Nothing in Scripture gives evidence that Joseph has become bitter and resentful as he easily might have. When the opportunity finally arrives he is not tangled in emotional baggage that would interfere with his rising to the occasion.

Prayerful Pause
May I offer God my grievances for healing so that I may serve with a clean and open heart.

Meditation 18

"You shall eat the fruit of the labor of your hands; you shall be happy, and it shall go well with you."
Psalm 128:2

Pharaoh is pleased and turns to those about him, saying "Can we find anyone else like this—one in whom is the spirit of God?" Within the course of a few hours, Joseph goes from the dungeon he has inhabited for years to the second in command in Egypt with responsibilities for the welfare of the entire country. What a meteoric rise to stardom! He wears the signet ring of the king, garments of fine linen, and a gold chain around his neck. He rides in the chariot of the second-in-command and people cry out "Bow the knee" as he passes by. And Pharaoh gives him a wife, the daughter of the priest of On.

Joseph's position certainly seems secure now and his new life clearly established. But perhaps at night in his dreams, or in unexpected moments during the day, he recalls the family of his youth. Is his father still alive? What has happened to his brothers, especially little Benjamin? Will he ever see them again, or at least have some word of them?

Sacred Ponderings
Joseph lives in prison for a long time, is suddenly released, given huge responsibility facing an oncoming famine, yet he still has some unresolved circumstances in his past. What are the lessons contained in this story for me about living in the present moment?

Prayerful Pause
Dear God, help me resolve whatever I can from my past that holds me back; treasure the good memories; face whatever the future holds courageously; steadfastly hold to my faith and live joyfully in the present moment.

Dreams Revisited

Genesis 41:46–42:17

"...When Joseph learned that there was grain in Egypt, he said to his sons, 'Why do you keep looking at one another? I have heard,' he said, 'that there is grain in Egypt; go down and buy grain for us there, that we may live and not die.' So ten of Joseph's brothers went down to buy grain in Egypt. But Jacob did not send Joseph's brother, Benjamin, with his brothers, for he feared that harm might come to him. Thus the sons of Israel were among the other people who came to buy grain, for the famine had reached the land of Canaan.

"Now Joseph was governor over the land; it was he who sold to all the people of the land. And Joseph's brothers came and bowed themselves before him with their faces to the ground. When Joseph saw his brothers, he recognized them, but he treated them like strangers and spoke harshly to them. 'Where do you come from?' he said. They said, 'From the land of Canaan, to buy food.' Although Joseph had recognized his brothers, they did not recognize him. Joseph also remembered the dreams that he had dreamed about them. He said to them, 'You are spies; you have come to see the nakedness of the land!' They said, 'We, your servants, are twelve brothers, the sons of a certain man in the land of Canaan; the youngest, however, is now with our father, and one is no more. But Joseph said to them, 'It is just as I have said to you; you are spies! Here is how you shall be tested; as Pharaoh lives, you shall not leave this place unless your youngest brother comes here! Let one of you go and bring your brother, while the rest of you remain in prison, in order that your words may be tested, whether there is truth in you...."

Meditation 19

"Hard times, come again no more."
—Stephen Foster

    Joseph enjoys seven years of plenty in the land. He is busy travelling through all the land of Egypt, storing up food in every city. There is such abundance that he can no longer measure it. During this time, Joseph also fathers two sons: Manasseh, meaning "God has made me forget all my hardship and all my father's house" and Ephraim, meaning "For God has made me fruitful in the land of my misfortunes."

    Joseph is a hard worker. But he lives with all the comforts of the Pharaoh's court, what we gather to be a happy marriage and the comfort and pleasure of his children. He is well regarded throughout the land as a wise and thoughtful leader who embodies the spirit of God. And yet it is hard to miss the yearning that comes through in the naming of his children. Has he really forgotten all his father's house or fully recovered from the misfortunes he experienced?

Sacred Ponderings

How many times has Joseph brought his family to God in prayer, praying for each of them, for their wellbeing as individuals and as a family? Many times we suppose, especially as the famine begins to become a reality.

Prayerful Pause

Even in those times when my life is full of joy and running smoothly, may I remember those, both known and unknown to me, who face the most difficult of circumstances.

Meditation 20

"The web of our life is a mingled yarn, good and ill together."
—Shakespeare

So the years of abundance come to an end and the famine ensues. Egypt and all the surrounding countries are affected. But Egypt is prepared. Joseph opens the storehouses to sell the people the grain that has been set aside through the previous years for just this moment. Some of the people panic but Pharaoh assures them to go to Joseph and do whatever he tells them to do. Joseph's wise preparations allow him to sell even to the surrounding countries, which are desperate.

While Joseph certainly has plenty to occupy his time and attention during this period, he may entertain the notion that his family back home is being affected and perhaps will seek help. And, in fact, when Jacob does hear the rumor that grain is available in Egypt, he seems to scold his sons. Essentially he says, "Quit acting so helpless and do something. Go to Egypt and get us some supplies."

He directs Joseph's ten older brothers to go, perhaps for safety in numbers. In times of scarcity, crime tends to increase. He fears to send Benjamin, the only child left to him from his marriage to Rebekah. He cannot in his wildest dreams imagine how this mission on which he sends his sons will unfold.

Sacred Ponderings
Thus far, we have seen Joseph recognize and utilize opportunities unlike his brothers who choose impulsive, reckless paths (selling Joseph, concocting a lie to tell their father) or who become immobilized in the face of difficult circumstances.

Prayerful Pause
May I be more like Joseph seeking constructive solutions to problems, avoiding reckless decisions or immobility.

Meditation 21

"Their hope is in him who saves them."
Sirach 34:15b

Since Joseph governs the process of dispensing grain, it is to Joseph that his brothers must present themselves. They are foreigners at the mercy of this man of considerable power. Nevertheless, they certainly are not prepared for his response to them. He recognizes them immediately. But they are clueless as to his identity.

While Joseph's response seems spiteful—indeed, the Scripture reads that "Joseph remembered his dreams that he had dreamed about them" and undoubtedly their response to those dreams—he must feel the need to see if they have matured through the years. This is also an opportunity, while they are still unaware who he is, to get the information he has longed to know.

Joseph accuses them of being spies. They are horrified and adamantly deny this. But they are put in prison for no just cause, just as Joseph was. For three days they remain in prison uncertain of their fate. No amount of scheming will get them out of this situation! Surely it must occur to them that their father, whom they have watched suffer for all these years over the loss of Joseph, may now starve to death, along with Benjamin. Heartsick, helpless, perhaps they call on God and pray for safe return to their father and their brother.

Sacred Ponderings
We all have choices how we respond to those who have wronged us.

Prayerful Pause
Dear God, may I always stay aware that I, too, have wronged others, when I contemplate responding to wrongs that are done to me.

Dreams Revisited

Genesis 42:18-38

"On the third day Joseph said to them, 'Do this and you will live, for I fear God: if you are honest men, let one of your brothers stay here where you are imprisoned. The rest of you shall go and carry grain for the famine of your households, and bring your youngest brother to me. Thus your words will be verified, and you shall not die.' And they agreed to do so. They said to one another, 'Alas, we are paying the penalty for what we did to our brother....'"

Meditation 22

"...and when you have sinned, repent." Sirach 18:21b

By the third day, the mood of the prison cell holding Joseph's brothers varies; sometimes frantic, sometimes remorseful, sometimes prayerful and definitely increasingly somber. But finally on that day they are brought before Joseph and he tells them that if they are honest men, they are to let one brother remain incarcerated while the others carry grain for the famine back to their homeland. At this point, this sounds like a huge improvement over what they have imagined their fate might be. But their renewed hope is quickly punctured when they are told that they must return with their youngest brother as a test of their veracity "so that you will not die."

They agree to this, but amongst themselves they despair, blaming their desperate circumstances as punishment for their mistreatment of Joseph so many years ago. Reuben cannot resist reminding them that he had, in fact, warned them not to harm Joseph. "You would not listen," Reuben says, "so now there is a reckoning for his blood."

To help maintain his anonymity, Joseph has carried on his conversations with them through an interpreter. Thus the brothers remain unaware that Joseph understands every word they are saying. As he hears their recriminations of one another and their recognition that their ill treatment of him is bearing a severe penalty, he is overcome with emotion, turns from them and weeps. Perhaps they are so caught up in their own emotions that they don't sense what is going on with Joseph. But one wonders if at least one of them doesn't pause long enough to think "What is that all about?"

Joseph composes himself, returns to them and picks Simeon to be held back and has him bound before their eyes.

Sacred Ponderings

One might think through the years that Joseph's brothers would have repented of their sin against Joseph but even now they seem to be anguishing more about the consequences that they are presently suffering. How long does it take me to acknowledge my wrongdoings and repent of them? Do I wait until the result catches up with me?

Prayerful Pause

May I take stock this very moment of those things "both done and undone" that need my action and God's grace.

Meditation 23

"If you have tears, prepare to shed them now."
—William Shakespeare

Joseph now orders that his brothers be supplied with grain and given provisions for their journey. Unbeknownst to them, he also orders that the money they brought to pay for the grain be returned to their sacks. One can only imagine the terror that strikes when they stop for the night and, in getting fodder for the donkeys, one of them discovers his money is in his sack. This trip is turning into a nightmare. They lose heart and begin trembling. They must surely imagine they have been set up to be found out as spies just as Joseph has accused them.

They are returning to their father minus Simeon and have yet to deliver the message to their father that to retrieve Simeon they must return with Benjamin. And now they also have to return to Egypt to face the possibility that they will be treated as spies and thieves. Scripture does not describe how they sleep that night but likely not well. Fragments of Joseph's dreams they had dismissed, images of his being carried off with slave traders to Egypt because of their own willingness to sacrifice him, fears of retribution, may well have disrupted the sleep of the weary, fearful travelers.

Sacred Ponderings
How often do I "lose heart" when circumstances are in a downward spiral?
What does it take to remind me of God's faithfulness?

Prayerful Pause
God when I have to "face the music" of events in my life, help me to face them with the awareness of Your loving presence.

Meditation 24

"A stubborn mind will be burdened by troubles."
Sirach 3:27a

    The trip home is mostly silent, broken occasionally by agonizing over facing their father, knowing that to convince him that they must bring Benjamin back with them is almost certainly going to be met with resistance, if not outright refusal. When they arrive, they give an accounting of their experience, noting immediately that "the lord of the land spoke harshly to us and charged us with spying on the land." (Translation: You see, Dad, what we had to go through just to get this food back here to you.) Perhaps they hope this will put their father on notice of the seriousness of the request they are about to make. They tell him about having to leave Simeon and how they were instructed to bring back Benjamin. But in the midst of this conversation they suddenly discover that all of them have had their money returned to their sacks! This is even worse than they thought!
    This seems to be the final straw for their father. Jacob is adamant that he will not send them back with Benjamin. He has lost too much already—Joseph and now Simeon. He will not dare risk sending Benjamin. Reuben makes a desperate attempt to get their father's cooperation, offering that Jacob can kill Reuben's two sons if Reuben does not bring Benjamin back to him. But Jacob's mind is made up. Nothing, not the hope of Simeon's safe return, not the promise of being able to trade freely in Egypt and avoid starvation, nothing can persuade Jacob to change his mind.

Sacred Ponderings
Have I ever stubbornly resisted something in my best interest because I feared the risk of taking action?

Prayerful Pause
Dear God, keep me aware of those times when I am stubborn, that I may examine if I am avoiding something important that You are calling me to do.

Dreams Dismantled

Genesis 43:1–44:13

Now the famine was severe in the land. And when they had eaten up the grain that they had brought from Egypt, their father said to them, 'Go again, buy us a little more food.' But Judah said to him, 'The man solemnly warned us, saying, 'You shall not see my face unless your brother is with you.... "Then their father Israel said to them, 'If it must be so, then do this: take some of the choice fruits of the land in your bags, and carry them down as a present to the man—a little balm and a little honey, gum, resin, pistachio nuts, and almonds. Take double the money with you. Carry back with you the money that was returned in the top of your sacks; perhaps it was an oversight."

Meditation 25

"Do not hide your face from your servant, for I am in distress."
Psalm 69:17a

Eventually, the food they brought from Egypt runs out. Jacob tells his sons to go back to Egypt to purchase more. Apparently Reuben has given up dealing with his father or is no longer able to. Now Judah intercedes. He reminds his father that the directions were quite explicit that they were not to return without their brother Benjamin. Jacob is irate that they even mentioned Benjamin at all. Why did the authority in Egypt have any reason to know about him? But Judah appeals to his father that they were simply cooperating with the man's questions and had no reason to believe he would require them to bring Benjamin to Egypt.

Judah tries a different approach with his father. If Jacob won't allow Benjamin to go, then the brothers simply will not make the trip. End of discussion. He assures his father that he can hold him accountable. He doesn't miss the opportunity to remind his father that if he had not balked to begin with they could have been back to Egypt for supplies several times by now.

Wearily, Jacob consents to allow Benjamin to go. He instructs his sons to take double the money that was in their bags, in order to return what was left in them and have money to buy grain. He also wants them to take some gifts to this ruler in Egypt, who has made such accusations against them and made such unusual demands. He prays for God's mercy on them, reminding them how bereft he is and how much he fears more loss.

Sacred Ponderings
Judah's determination and willingness to be accountable is the first sign that perhaps the dynamics are shifting in the family. What shifts might I make in my own life to create needed change?

Prayerful Pause
Dear God, grant me courage to make whatever changes, take whatever risks are necessary to follow Your guidance.

Meditation 26

"My heart is like wax; it is melted within my breast."
Psalm 22:14b

The brothers make their way to Egypt and are brought before Joseph at his house. All the anxieties that have built up over the course of this journey come to a head. They believe they have been brought to Joseph's residence because of the money that was replaced in their sacks and that they are almost surely about to be put into slavery. They are fearful for their wellbeing. They also hear the echo of their father's final words to them: "As for me, if I am bereaved of my children, I am bereaved."

They quickly make explanation about the money and offer it back along with the money for more grain. But they are reassured that everything is okay. Then Simeon is brought out to them. They make ready their gifts to present to Joseph at the meal they understand he is going to be sharing with them. When Joseph arrives, they bow down to him. Then he inquires after their father's health. He notices Benjamin and asks if this is their youngest brother. At the sight of Benjamin, Joseph once again is filled with emotion and leaves the room. Perhaps the brothers whisper to one another about what the meaning this behavior has. Yet nothing indicates that even now they have any inkling of Joseph's identity.

Joseph weeps privately, washes his face and returns with orders for the meal to be served. They are unable to actually eat with Joseph because the Egyptians consider eating with Hebrews to be an abomination. But they are served portions from Joseph's table. They are astounded when Benjamin's portions are five times as much as any of theirs. Yet another clue to the mystery of this ruler! But, making no sense of it, they simply relax from their hair-raising experience and drink and are "merry" with him.

Sacred Ponderings
Am I willing to let go of what I don't understand and be joyful in the moment?

Prayerful Pause
Dear God, too often I am so busy trying to "figure things out" that I miss the opportunity simply to "be." Help me to take a break from analyzing and "be merry."

Meditation 27

"For gold is tested in the fire, and those found acceptable, in the furnace of humiliation." Sirach 2:5

Joseph has yet to fully trust that his brothers understand their wrongdoing, are repentant and worthy of trust. We can ponder the cruelty of these continued tests from someone with such power over his brothers' lives. But on further reflection, he does not appear to be toying with them, but giving them the opportunity to develop as individuals and as a family. Their early life together was marked by resentments and conflict. Can they now come together and work through difficulties for the good of the entire family?

Joseph has the men's sacks filled with food and money. But this time when he sends them on their way he has put his silver cup in the top of Benjamin's sack. Once again the brothers start back home, the beginning of a joyful trip. They savor the memory of dinner with the ruler Joseph and relish the satisfaction of having plenty of grain. Even better, they have Simeon and Benjamin safely in their company. Their poor father will be overwhelmed with relief and gratitude. Perhaps they will have redeemed themselves with their father, whose grief they have witnessed daily all these years.

But wait! The steward overtakes them when they have gone only a short distance and declares that they have stolen the ruler's silver cup. They are utterly astounded. Are their fortunes once again to be reversed? They remind the steward that they brought money back that they thought was not rightfully theirs. Why would they steal the silver cup? They say that should that be so, the one with the cup should die and the rest become slaves. The steward replies that the one with the cup shall become a slave and the rest are free to return home. Starting with the eldest's bag, he begins the search, ending with Benjamin's bag, where the cup is discovered. The brothers tear their clothes as a measure of their agitation and distress. Now they all head back together to the city.

Sacred Ponderings

Life takes some unexpected, sometimes dreadful, turns. Do I find opportunities to strengthen kinships/friendships with those who "put skin on God "during those times?

Prayerful Pause

May I ever remember that crisis is opportunity for growth and development of inner strength and outward connection.

Dreams Resurrected

Genesis 44:14–45:15

"Judah and his brothers came to Joseph's house while he was still there; and they fell to the ground before him. Joseph said to them, 'What deed is this that you have done? Do you not know that one such as I can practice divination?' And Judah said, 'What can we say to my lord? What can we speak? How can we clear ourselves? God has found out the guilt of your servants; here we are then, my lord's slaves, both we and also the one in whose possession the cup has been found.' But he said, 'Far be it from me that I should do so! Only the one in whose possession the cup was found shall be my slave; but as for you go up in peace to your father....'

"Then Joseph could no longer control himself before all those who stood by him, and he cried out, 'Send everyone away from me.' So no one stayed with him when Joseph made himself known to his brothers. And he wept so loudly that the Egyptians heard it, and the household of Pharaoh heard it. Joseph said to his brothers, 'I am Joseph. Is my father still alive?' But his brothers could not answer him, so dismayed were they at his presence."

Meditation 28

"From you let my vindication come. Let your eyes see the right."
Psalm 17:2

The "silver cup" which has ended up in Benjamin's sack at Joseph's direction is not just any cup. The Egyptians had influenced the Israelites with "divination," a method of seeking to discern the future and the cup was an instrument of "divination." When Joseph's siblings return he reminds them that they have been found with this item important to the kingdom. At a loss as to how else to handle this serious situation in which they find themselves, they simply admit, "What can we say to my lord? What can we speak? How can we clear ourselves?" They declare themselves guilty and offer themselves as servants.

The "method" to Joseph's "madness" becomes more evident. He states that only Benjamin, in whose possession the cup has been found, must remain as a servant. The rest are free to go. The question for him is clear: will they again sacrifice a brother?

The Scripture reflects no hesitation on Judah's part: "O my lord, let your servant please speak words in my lord's ears, and do not be angry." He recounts how they had to convince their father to part with another child and he pleads his father's case for the return of Benjamin. He offers to be a slave in Benjamin's stead. One can only begin to imagine the mix of emotion in that room as this conversation unfolds: Judah intensely focused and urgently persistent; Joseph holding his breath to see if the change he so hopes has occurred, in fact has; Benjamin, feeling torn because he is the object of this tug of war and also very aware of the impact on his father if he doesn't return; the other siblings awaiting the outcome with clenched hearts and bated breath. Others in the room must be puzzled at Joseph's behavior and have been all along, grasping that something very significant is going on, yet clueless as to the nature of it.

Sacred Ponderings
When have I pled the cause of someone or something, because it was the right thing to do—even if it meant risking my own wellbeing? Would I show the courage of Judah?

Prayerful Pause
Dear God, help me to be aware of opportunities and be willing to take up a just cause, even when there is clear risk in doing so. Amen

Meditation 29

*"If the great Lord is willing, his heart will be filled with
the spirit of understanding."*
Sirach 39:6

What a climactic moment! Joseph can bear it no longer. He cries out, "Send everyone away from me!" His attendants, mystified, scurry out. The entire palace must be in a state of high alert! What is going on? Has Joseph lost his senses? Why do these Israelites seeking food have such an impact on him? Is he safe? Do they need to be prepared to rescue him? By now Joseph's history as a slave brought by traders to Egypt is an obscure memory. That truth has been eclipsed by his astounding rise in the kingdom.

Joseph weeps so loudly that all the household of Pharaoh hears it. Perhaps some ears were cupped to the door as Joseph reveals to his brothers, at last, "I am Joseph. Is my father still alive?" Suddenly the brothers begin to connect the dots, how Joseph has tested them repeatedly to ascertain if they have grown beyond their self-centered and quarrelsome ways. But they are too stunned to respond. They feel like they are standing before a ghost, the brother they have assumed likely never survived servitude. Relief, guilt, fear all surface in rapid succession.

Sacred Ponderings

Sometimes we are witnesses to confounding events. Imagine those in the household as they begin to grasp what has happened. Some will be thrilled for Joseph's reconnection with his family. Some will grumble that the brothers should get the punishment they so richly deserve. How might I have responded?

Prayerful Pause

God, grant me the openness of spirit to rejoice with those who rejoice and to weep with those who weep.

Meditation 30

"Love covers all offences."
Proverbs 12b

Joseph says to his brothers, "Come closer to me." Spellbound, they approach him. He offers the most healing words they could possibly hope to hear, encouraging them not to be distressed or to be angry with themselves, that God sent him into this situation "to preserve for you a remnant on earth, and to keep alive for you many survivors." And, then, he lavishes more good news upon them. They are to go home and get their father and they and their children and grandchildren and flocks are all to come to Egypt where he will provide for them throughout the period of famine. Joseph embraces Benjamin and they both weep. Then he kisses all his brothers, still weeping. At last they begin to converse openly with one another.

Imagine the trip home to retrieve their father and their families and belongings: "Remember those dreams Joseph had? They just seemed so impossible and arrogant. And now we discover they were true all along!" "I always wanted to believe he was still alive, but it just didn't seem possible."

"How did he ever forgive us?" "God is so good to have brought Joseph through this in such a marvelous way and to give him such a kind and generous spirit towards us."

Sacred Ponderings
How often in the midst of troubles we forget we are on God's marvelous journey and we never know just where God will take us.

Prayerful Pause
Thank you, God, for all the times you have brought me through difficulties, some I thought I could not possibly bear; and for your constancy, even when I am so burdened I don't notice it.

Epilogue

Genesis 45:16–46:7 & 46:28–47:12

"The land of Egypt is before you; settle your father and your brothers in the best part of the land."—Pharaoh
Genesis 47:6

Amidst the good news is one apparent problem. Shepherds are abhorrent to the Egyptians. Joseph approaches Pharaoh about this situation, as sheepherding is all his brothers have ever done. He selects five of his brothers to go before Pharaoh where, when asked, "What is your occupation?" they respond, "Your servants are shepherds, as our ancestors were." Have they come this far only to be sent back? But, no! Pharaoh says "The land of Egypt is before you." He even offers them the best part of the land.

Of course, this is not the end of the story. The Israelites have many more twists and turns of burden and blessing ahead of them. Our stories are never ended. We are always on a journey with God. Thank God, we do not journey alone. Grace is always available. And, as Joseph's experience has shown us, we can become participants in God's dreams. May we all seek to be God's dreamers, working on behalf of peace and justice for all God's people—a dream in progress.

Sacred Ponderings
Am I in touch with the awesome opportunity to be one of "God's dreamers"?

Prayerful Pause
Dear God, place deep within me the desire to seek the peace, justice, and mercy characteristic of Your intent for the world.

Our Story Evolves

God's Spirit Prevails in Human Weakness

The Story Begins: 1 Samuel 1:1-18: *"Now there was a certain man from Ramathaim, a Zuphite from the highlands of Ephraim, whose name was Elkanah. He was from the tribe of Ephraim, and he was the son of Jeroham son of Elihu son of Tohu of Zuph. Elkanah had two wives, one named Hannah and the other named Peninnah. Peninnah had children, but Hannah didn't...."*

Meditation 1

1 Samuel 1:1-18

Hannah speaks: Another day of taunts from Peninnah. My heart breaks. Soon it will be time to go again up to Shiloh to offer sacrifice. How can I bear this? My Lord God, how long must I suffer this way?

The story of Israel's transformation from loose tribal affiliations to the tradition of kings begins with a barren woman. Hannah is the much loved wife of Elkanah—and the much resented rival for his affections by his other wife Peninnah. Hannah's misery is quite evident as the same scenario is played out every year at the annual trip to the Israelite sanctuary at Shiloh, a major place of worship of the Israelite tribes and the resting place for the "ark of God" at this time. Peninnah gets the greater portion of the sacrifice for herself and her sons and daughters. Hannah gets only a small portion. Peninnah ridicules her. Hannah cries and won't eat...until the year when she's had enough.

This particular year, after the meal Hannah leaves to present herself to the Lord. Upset and crying, she silently pleads with God to give her a son and makes a solemn promise that she will give this child to the Lord for his entire life. He will be a Nazarite, "one made holy or separate" and no razor will ever touch his head.

The chief priest, witnessing her lips moving but not speaking, assumes she is drunk. Sober up, he warns her. Hannah protests, "I'm just a very sad woman. I haven't had any wine or beer but have been pouring out my heart to the Lord." Realizing his mistake, Eli blesses her: "Then go in peace. And may the God of Israel give you what you've asked from him." Hannah goes on her way—and is no longer sad.

Sacred Ponderings
When has something mattered so much to me that I poured all the longing of my heart out to God?

Prayerful Pause
O God, may I always, as Hannah, be willing to trust You with my deepest emotions.

Meditation 2

1 Samuel 1:19-28

Hannah speaks: I am not ready to take him to the temple. I will wean him and then he can be presented to the Lord to stay there permanently. I will offer him as a Nazarite forever. **Elkanah speaks:** Do what seems best to you. But remember what you have promised.

Soon after returning from the temple, Hannah's hope, Eli's blessing, are fulfilled! Hannah conceives and gives birth to Samuel, a name meaning "God has heard." The family constellation is reconfigured, Peninnah's tongue falls silent. But when it is time to go on the annual trek to the temple, Hannah is insistent that she will not be going. All these years of waiting to conceive! All the joy of at last having this child in her arms, at her breast. No, she is not going. But she promises that when Samuel is weaned she will indeed take him to the temple in order to live there permanently. He will serve the priest and live as a Nazarite. Fortunately, Elkanah doesn't make an issue of this and tells her to do as she sees fit. But he gently reminds her that she made this promise to God and it is still her duty to fulfill it.

Samuel, finally weaned and still quite young, is taken by Hannah to the temple, along with offerings of a young bull, an ephah of flour and a jar of wine. The bull is slaughtered and the offerings and Samuel are presented to Eli. Imagine the pleasure it gives Hanna to say to Eli: "Excuse me, sir! As surely as you live, sir, I am the woman who stood there next to you, praying to the Lord. I prayed for this boy, and the Lord gave me what I asked from him. So now I give this boy back to the Lord. As long as he lives, he is given to the Lord." And then the family worshipped together.

Sacred Ponderings
What have I longed for so much that I made promises to God, in hopes to persuade God to hear and answer? Did I keep those promises?

Prayerful Pause
O God, when I offer my longing to you, may I do so with an open heart, willing to receive whatever you make known to me.

Meditation 3

1 Samuel 2:1-10

Hannah speaks: My heart rejoices in the Lord!

One might surmise that Hannah felt painful pangs of parting from her little son. The temple was hardly "next door" where she might see him at any time. But she chooses to handle whatever emotions she is experiencing through the act of praising God. Hannah's song, similar to Mary's Magnificat centuries later, is a beautiful tribute to God, to the ways in which God empowers the powerless. Just as Hannah once felt powerless in her barren condition but relied on God's grace, allowing God to work in her life, Israel is in the midst of God's transformative power. The loose tribal affiliations will be replaced with kingship. And Samuel will play a significant role in this transformation.

Hannah's song gives recognition to her own experience ("My mouth mocks my enemies because I rejoice in your deliverance!" Listen up, Peninnah! Pay attention you nations about us who heckle Israel!) and also points towards the future ("May God give strength to his king and raise high the strength of his anointed one.") Thus begins the story of an unfolding future for Samuel in the temple serving Eli and for Israel as well.

Sacred Ponderings
When my emotions are swirling within me, how often do I turn to praise and thanksgiving?

Prayerful Pause
Dear God, grant me the wisdom to seek you out in the midst of change and to offer my gratitude even before the outcome is evident.

Meditation 4

1 Samuel 2:12-17

The priest's assistant speaks: "Give the priest some meat to roast. He won't accept boiled meat from you."

How is it that Eli's sons don't know the Lord, one wonders. They have grown up in the temple with their father the priest. We know nothing of their experiences there. We have no mention of their mother. We are told their names are Hophni and Phinehas. And we know they are considered despicable—likely by everyone who witnesses their behavior, including their father who apparently feels helpless to intervene in any meaningful way.

Were they fulfilling their duties in the prescribed method, they would wait for the meat to be cooked in the proper way; to be boiled first, then burned and, following the required sacrifice, to be shared as a communal meal. In their greed, they take meat while it is still raw, so they can prepare it more to their liking. But this deprives worshippers of offering their best sacrifice to God. Hophni and Phinehas make a farce of the offerings of sacrifice, a very serious offense as it is most disrespectful towards God.

Sacred Ponderings
It is easy to judge Eli's sons harshly, as their behavior was unacceptable in so many ways: disrespectful towards their father, towards others, towards God, even towards themselves. But if we examine ourselves closely, we are likely to find areas where our own behavior has been less than exemplary.

Prayerful Pause
Dear God, help me to take the "beam" out of my own eye and be less concerned with the "moat" in someone else's. Amen.

Meditation 5

1 Samuel 2:18-21

Eli speaks: "May the Lord replace the child of this woman that you gave back to the Lord."

Into this situation with Eli's corrupt sons, the little child Samuel is delivered by his parents to the temple to assist Eli. Imagine Eli responsible for the care of a young child! This investment of Eli's time must leave even less time to supervise Hophni and Phinehas, but is clearly more rewarding.

Imagine young Samuel grasping that his parents are far away. Will he see them again? With so little understanding of time as a youngster, he must surely wonder. Each year, though, his mother and father show up, his mother bearing a linen priestly vest she has painstakingly worked on throughout the year for her dear child whom she misses so. Perhaps these long-anticipated visits are a little awkward as so much time elapses between them. Both geographically and practically, their everyday lives are so distant from one another. But perhaps a kind of rhythm develops over the years as Samuel matures.

And he most certainly is maturing. While Elkanah and Hannah are busy at home with the siblings of Samuel, three brothers and two sisters, "God's replacements" as it were, scripture reports Samuel to be "growing up in the Lord's service."

Sacred Ponderings
There are times when we feel as abandoned as a small child in an unfamiliar world. What resources do we call on? Where do we turn?

Prayerful Pause
O, God, remind me I am not alone.

Meditation 6

1 Samuel 2:22-36

A man of God speaks to Eli: "I chose your father from all of Israel's tribes to be my priest. Why then do you kick my sacrifices and my offerings—the very ones I commanded for my dwelling place? Why do you respect your sons more than me? You'll see trouble in my dwelling place, though all will go well for Israel. And what happens to your two sons Hophni and Phinehas will be a sign for you: they will both die on the same day. Then I will establish for myself a trustworthy priest who will act in accordance with my thoughts and desires."

The "man of God," who speaks as a prophet to Eli, brings an unmistakable message: God has had enough! This deliberate, defiant disrespect, this blatant exploitation of the people's offerings and of the office of the priesthood itself will no longer be tolerated. Israel will survive intact, but Eli's family's role to carry the priestly duties is forever altered.

Surely Eli has had some expectation that judgment would be coming. He has watched his sons as their behavior deteriorated and the priesthood unraveled at the seams of their priestly vestments. This could not go on endlessly. There will be consequences. Eli may in some sense be relieved that at last there is some intervention here. Their intolerable actions, which he had seemed helpless to effectively address, are being brought to a screeching halt, an undignified end to their undignified behavior.

Sacred Ponderings
When has my own behavior brought consequences I did not, or chose not to, see coming? How did I handle the consequences?

Prayerful Pause
O God, when I use poor judgement, when I suffer for unethical or unbecoming behavior on my part, may I turn to you, seek forgiveness, and return to your path.

Meditation 7

1 Samuel 3:1-10

The narrator speaks: "Now the boy Samuel was serving the Lord under Eli. The Lord's word was rare at that time and visions weren't widely known."

What a telling description of the circumstances at the time Samuel is growing up in the temple! Eli's fading eyesight seems to reflect both the reality of his diminished physical capacities and to speak metaphorically of his dramatically reduced spiritual vision. However, the scripture tells us "God's light hadn't gone out yet." And, indeed, Eli does maintain enough sense of God's spirit to recognize God's call to Samuel.

Samuel lies asleep in "the Lord's temple," a tent sanctuary where he likely has some duties. Quite symbolically, he sleeps next to "God's chest," the Ark of the Covenant, the symbol of God's presence. Imagine Samuel, awakened from sleep, knowing Eli is old and may be in distress, thinking Eli is calling to him out of some need for help. But he checks on Eli, who denies having called to him. Samuel drifts back into sleep. But once again he hears his name called, returns to Eli, who repeats that he has not called Samuel, perhaps suggests to Samuel that he was dreaming. Samuel returns to bed, feeling confused. When he hears his name yet a third time, he feels compelled to return to Eli for one more check on him. As anyone who has been awakened in the night having heard something from an unidentifiable source, he may investigate nooks and crannies on his way to Eli's room.

This time, though, the aging Eli has the wisdom to realize this is God seeking Samuel. He instructs Samuel to say: "Speak, Lord. Your servant is listening." Samuel dutifully returns and follows Eli's advice.

Sacred Ponderings
Am I paying attention for God's voice in my life or will it be necessary for God to shake me awake to listen? Will I then recognize God's voice and how will I respond if I do?

Prayerful Pause
Nudge me awake, O God. May I recognize your voice in my life and respond to those things to which you call me.

Meditation 8

1 Samuel 3:11-4:1

The Lord speaks: "I am about to do something in Israel…"

What might Samuel be wondering, there in the darkness, awaiting what message God will convey to him? He has been a faithful servant to Eli, fulfilled his duties, been the very offering to God his mother had hoped and presented him to be. But to be called by name, in the night? Whatever sort of task might God be setting out? It is easy to believe he might be thinking "Am I ready for this??"

And what he hears is indeed daunting! God says "I am about to do something in Israel that will make the ears of all who hear it tingle!" He goes on to say, among other things, that Eli's family's wrongdoing "will never be reconciled by sacrifice or offering." Samuel lies wide awake till dawn, dreading to relay to Eli what God has said, knowing that Eli will certainly ask.

Eli, to his credit, is adamant that Samuel must be honest and tell him everything God said. Samuel hides nothing from him and Eli accepts this judgment, perhaps with an air of resignation. If he had any faint hope of some reprieve, it is clear one is not coming.

From this point on, Samuel's reputation only grows as a competent and holy person of God. All of Israel, scripture tells us, recognize him as trustworthy. God continues to speak to him and Samuel acts as God's messenger to the people.

Sacred Ponderings
When have I questioned, "Am I ready for this?"

Prayerful Pause
Dear God, May I be empowered by your calling instead of paralyzed by my fear. Amen.

Meditation 9

1 Samuel 4:2-22

The narrator speaks: "In those days the Philistines gathered for war against Israel."

The Philistines are no small threat. Situated on the southeastern coastal plain adjacent to central and southern Israel, they are well organized and have professional military forces…and kings! No doubt Israel's clamoring for a king was related to the encroachment they felt from this powerful and menacing people. Their loose tribal alliances were no match for these folks!

Having been defeated in the first round of battle, the Israelites decide that their best bet is to take the Ark of the Covenant into battle. This chest, made under Moses' direction during the years the Israelites spent in the wilderness when they fled Egypt, carries the tablets with God's commandments in it. Surely, they conclude, this powerful symbol of God's presence can only bring them victory! Initially, the Philistines are frightened by the uproar created by the Israelites when they carry the ark to the battlefield. But then the great racquet only serves to strengthen the Philistines' resolve against the Israelites. It is a massive defeat, God's chest is captured and Hophni and Phineas are killed.

Eli, awaiting the news by the side of the road, keels over dead when it is delivered to him. The fate of his sons had been foretold. But the ark's loss is more than old Eli can take. And Phineas' wife goes into labor, birthing a baby boy whom, with her dying breath, she names Ichabod, meaning "the glory has gone out of Israel." Indeed, without the ark, Israel is bereft.

Sacred Ponderings
When have I, like the Israelites, felt so defeated that God's presence seems remote/inaccessible?

Prayerful Pause
O, God, even in loss, failure, defeat, disgrace, may I trust You are with me.

Meditation 10

1 Samuel 5:1–6:21

The narrator speaks: "Then the Philistines took God's chest and brought it into Dagon's temple."

As is customary for the victors in war, the Philistines take the Ark of the Covenant they had secured in battle and display it before the statue of their god Dagon. Surely the act is meant as a discount to the Israelites' God. But, wouldn't you know, the next morning the statue is found lying face down. The Philistines restore it to its rightful place, only to find it face down the next day, with head and hands broken off. And this is only the beginning of the Philistines troubles with God's chest!

One Philistine city after another tries taking the chest but each one in turn is stricken with a plague of tumors. They become desperate to get rid of the ark and to return it to Israel. Clearly the God of Israel has demonstrated divine power which is to be respected. So they decide not only to return the ark, but to make an offering to appease this mighty God.

Along with the Ark of the Covenant, in a cart pulled by two nursing cows, they load up "five gold tumors and gold mice" which we might speculate are representative of the disease itself and how they understand it was transmitted. The cows, separated from their calves, would be expected to return to their offspring. Instead the cows, in a demonstration of divine involvement, take the cart directly to Israelite territory where the people of Beth-Shemesh joyfully accept it.

Apparently, though, the sons of Jeconiah show some disrespect towards the Ark and 70 people are struck down as a result! The message clearly is that God's presence is holy and God's power is undeniable.

Sacred Ponderings
When did I last feel awed by God's presence and power?

Prayerful Pause
Dear God, renew my sense of wonder and keen awareness of Your Presence.
Amen.

Meditation 11

1 Samuel 7:2-6

The narrator speaks: "Now a long time passed—a total of twenty years—after the chest came to stay in Kiriath-Jearim, and the whole house of Israel yearned for the Lord."

Twenty years?? Once again, the scriptures omit some details, leaving us to our best imaginations. Recognizing humanity's tendency towards self-absorption and propensity for wandering away from God, we can easily consider that the Israelites have become more immersed in the culture around them. But at some point a longing for God begins to be awakened within them.

Samuel takes this opportunity to encourage them: "If you are turning to the Lord with all your heart, then get rid of all the foreign gods and the astartes you have. Set your heart on the Lord!" Why rid themselves of those gods? Consider Astarte: this goddess of fertility and reproduction in the Phoenician and Canaanite cultures plays a significant role in their lives. When the Israelites had arrived in Canaan, they had discovered a fertile land, unlike anything they had known. The Canaanites attributed this to their gods: Baal, son of Astarte (or Asherah) and to Astarte, considered both Baal's mother and his mistress. Astarte is worshipped in various ways, including ritual sex, believed to influence the gods to provide a good harvest.

This might have been a hard sell by anyone else. But Samuel demonstrates his considerable leadership skills, convincing them to assemble at Mizpah where he prays for them: they pour out water, acknowledging their need for repentance and cleansing; they fast and confess their sins.

Sacred Ponderings
When I look at my life, where have I become consumed with the culture, allowed myself to be distracted from God?

Prayerful Pause
Search me, O God, and know my thoughts. See if there be any wicked way in me. And lead me in the way everlasting. (Psalm 139:23-24)

Meditation 12

1 Samuel 7:7-14

The Israelites beg: "Please don't stop praying to the Lord our God for us."

Word travels fast and the Philistines become aware that Israel is gathered at Mizpah. This is interpreted by the Philistines as a sign of war. Panicked, the Israelites, not wanting another face off with this army, plead with Samuel to continue praying for them. So Samuel prepares a burnt offering and cries to the Lord on behalf of Israel. Even as Samuel is making the offering, the Philistines begin their advance. "But the Lord," scripture tells us, "thundered against the Philistines with a great blast."

So with a terrifying clap of thunder, the tide turns and the Israelites are pursuing the Philistines and the Philistines are roundly defeated! Samuel, in recognition of God's power and deliverance, erects a stone between Mizpah and Jeshanah, naming it "Ebenezer," meaning "stone of help." Samuel pointedly declares, "The Lord helped us to this very point."

The verses following would have us believe that the Philistines are defeated once and for all in this battle, when in fact it is until the time of David that their stranglehold on Israel is broken. But for the people of Israel, these verses reflect a resurrected awareness of God's power in their lives, a renewed sense of God's presence among them and of Samuel's capacity as their leader.

Sacred Ponderings
How often have we sung the lines "Here I raise my Ebenezer" with no thought to these verses?

Prayerful Pause
O God, here may we raise our Ebenezers, recognizing you have helped us "to this very point"—are present with us in this very moment and are our trusted companion as we journey onward.

Meditation 13

1 Samuel 7:15-17

The narrator speaks: "Samuel served as Israel's judge his whole life."

The little boy brought to the temple as a very young child, dedicated by his mother to the service of the temple and its priest Eli, has now served the people faithfully his entire life, travelling from Bethel to Gilgal to Mizpah, acting in the role of the wise judge on God's behalf. His journey always takes him back to Ramah, where he makes his home and establishes an altar. All of these towns are located in the midst of the tribe of Benjamin, from whom the first king of Israel will be chosen. But wait! A king for Israel? This has never been. Aren't things perfectly fine the way they are? Isn't God the king of Israel? These verses begin so peacefully: Samuel makes his appointed rounds, God's messenger dealing out justice with mercy. But they presage huge change on the horizon. Have "the wheels come off" from Israel? Can you feel the tension and anxiety rising?

Sacred Ponderings
Am I struggling with change in some area of my life? Is there some tension or anxiety I recognize related to change?

Prayerful Pause
When I am prone to cling to what no longer works, help me seek Your wisdom.

Meditation 14

1 Samuel 8:1-22

The Israelite elders speak: "Listen. You are old now, and your sons don't follow in your footsteps."

Whoa! Who wants to be told he is old? Or reminded of his children's bad behavior? Yes, he is old and yes, his sons that he appointed to serve as judges have been accepting bribes and perverting justice. While Samuel might have expected that there would be some outcry that he do something, given his sons' despicable performance in a divinely ordained role, this demand for kingship seems to totally catch him off guard. The elders have added insult to injury! One can almost imagine him walking away muttering to himself: "A king! Indeed! Haven't I served these people all my life and served them well? Well, I'll just take this matter up with God. "

Samuel prays to the Lord, almost surely expecting God's rebuke of the people for such an outrageous demand. But God responds with a surprising answer: "Comply with the people's request." God assures Samuel this is not a rejection of Samuel but of God. Samuel is to appoint a king, but he must also warn the people of some of the consequences they can expect from this action. Samuel thus gives the people all the worst case scenarios that can come with kingship.

The people still insist on having kingship "like all the other nations." In their defense, it is worth recognizing that Israel is occupied at this time by Philistines, who have kings in each of five cities. Those five kings are in alliance with one another, making for an ever-present threat.

Samuel talks to God again, gets the same answer, and likely in some frustration, tells the people "Go home now."

Sacred Ponderings
How do I deal with leaders whose leadership I find lacking? Have I been in roles of leadership myself when I have overlooked obvious problems or provided less than adequate guidance?

Prayerful Pause
O God, help me, as an imperfect person, to evaluate and address problems with a spirit that comes from being grounded in You, the Ground of All Being.

Meditation 15

1 Samuel 9:1-21

The narrator speaks: "No one in Israel was more handsome than Saul, and he stood head and shoulders above everyone else."

We do love our leaders to be handsome and tall! And, isn't it also typical, that our leaders like to focus on their humble beginnings. And thus, in a pattern we may recognize, the story unfolds of the choosing of the first king of Israel.

A wealthy man named Kish, from the tribe of Benjamin, has a son named Saul. In a seemingly rather ordinary circumstance, Kish sends Saul out with a servant to hunt for some lost donkeys. When the search seems futile, Saul is ready to go home. But the servant, maybe cleverly sensing the opportunity for a "lark," a diversion from his normal duties, says "Wait a minute…….there's a fellow there, a man of God, who foretells things that actually happen! Maybe he would know where the donkeys are!"

The scripture, often devoid of much detail, here is rich with small details about this journey. They determine what they can bring as a gift for the man of God. They encounter some young women and ask of them where they can find him. And into this apparently mundane story, scripture reveals: "Now the day before Saul came, the Lord had revealed to Samuel: About this time tomorrow I will send you a man from the Benjaminite territory. You will anoint him as leader of my people Israel. He will save them from the Philistines' power because I have seen the suffering of my people."

When Saul approaches Samuel, Samuel reveals himself to Saul as the "seer" he is seeking, invites him to dinner and tells him the donkeys have been located. Why should he worry about donkeys anyway, Samuel asks, since he comes from such a wealthy family? Oh no, Saul protests, I'm from the smallest family in the smallest tribe of Benjamin. Essentially Saul claims "I'm nobody!"

Sacred Ponderings
When have I dodged responsibility by claiming "I'm nobody! "

Prayerful Pause
O God, when I am called on for some task, may I prayerfully consider if it is mine to take on. And when Your calling comes as a surprise, may I open myself to the movement of Your Spirit.

Meditation 16

1 Samuel 9:22–10:9

The narrator speaks: "Then Samuel took Saul and his young servant and brought them to the banquet room. He gave them an honored place among the invited guests."

Samuel treats Saul as though he is already king! Saul, surely befuddled, doesn't consider himself due all this special attention. Samuel feeds him a special meal, eats with him, and makes accommodations for Saul for the night.

Near dawn, Samuel calls to Saul on the roof where he has been bedded down. Samuel is instructing him to wake up, and get ready to depart.

So Samuel accompanies Saul to the edge of town, where he directs Saul to dismiss his servant for the moment. "But you stop for a bit," he tells Saul, "so I can tell you God's word." Saul, wordlessly, complies.

Samuel takes a small jar of oil, pours it over Saul's head and kisses him. "The Lord hereby anoints you leader of his people Israel."

Saul is surely thinking this must be a case of mistaken identity! Samuel has mistaken him for someone else! But, no! Samuel promises him signs that will demonstrate the truth of what he has declared: he will meet men who confirm that the donkeys have been found; he will encounter men who offer him bread, which he is to accept; and he will see a band of prophets. The Lord's spirit will come over him and he will "become a completely different person."

True to Samuel's prediction, just as Saul turns to leave Samuel's side, God gives him a different heart, and all these signs happen the very same day.

Sacred Ponderings
"You do not need to know precisely what is happening or where it is all going. What you need is to recognize the possibilities and challenges offered by the present moment and to embrace them with courage, faith, and hope."
—Thomas Merton

Prayerful Pause
O, God, truly may I recognize "the possibilities and challenges offered by the present moment" and trust You in all the situations in my life which I cannot decipher. Amen.

Meditation 17

1 Samuel 10:10-16

The narrator speaks: "When Saul and the boy got to Gibeah, there was a group of prophets coming to meet him."

What a curious passage this is! With all that has occurred with Samuel, and with the new heart that has been bestowed upon him, Saul now encounters the group of prophets, and is overcome with the Spirit of Lord. Imagine the sounds of harps, tambourines, flutes and lyres…dancing…shouting…songs of praise…spontaneous prayers. We might imagine whirling dervishes or a modern day Pentecostal service. Whatever this entails, people who have known Saul say "What's happened to Kish's son?" No one knows what to make of this.

Saul himself is still processing the experience. When the intensity dies down, he goes home. Making conversation or perhaps sensing something dramatically different in Saul's persona, Saul's uncle asks, "Where did you go?"

Without skipping a beat, Saul cryptically replies: "To look for the donkeys, but when we couldn't find anything, we went to Samuel."

'Well, whatever did Samuel tell you?" his uncle asks, his interest piqued.

And Saul, who cannot yet bring himself to speak of what happened, merely says "He reassured me that the donkeys had been found." He omits all the dramatic details, does not tell his uncle one word about the kingship. The kingship! This is Big News… Does he think his uncle wouldn't believe him? Does he just want to live with this new understanding for a while until he comes to grip with this mystery?

Sacred Ponderings

Much as Mary "kept all these things and pondered them in her heart," sometimes the mysteries, the miracles in our own lives are best considered privately, while other times we are wise to share them with trusted confidantes.

Prayerful Pause

O, God, may I recognize and value the sometimes puzzling gifts in my own life. May I listen for Your wisdom as I ponder them. Amen.

Meditation 18

1 Samuel 10:17-22

Samuel speaks to the Israelites whom he has summoned to Mizpah: "This is what the Lord God of Israel says: I brought you up out of Egypt, and I delivered you from the Egyptians' power and from the power of all the kingdoms that oppressed you. But today you have rejected your God who saved you from all your troubles and difficulties by saying, 'No! Appoint a king over us!'"

It is impossible to read this without hearing the distress in Samuel's voice. He then instructs the people to come forward by their tribes and clans, and begins a system perhaps similar to casting lots. He selects the tribe of Benjamin (the smallest of the twelve tribes of Israel) and from that tribe, the family of Mari is chosen. He goes through the family one by one.

Scripture does not convey the drama that is surely going on. They have asked for a king! It is to be one from among them…You can almost hear the murmurings among them: Will our family be the one that houses the one to be king over Israel? The hush falls as Samuel selects…Saul! But wait! Where IS Saul?

In a most inauspicious beginning, Saul is hiding among the supplies!

Sacred Ponderings
When have I blanched at a critical moment, been unavailable when I was most needed?

Prayerful Pause
O God, when I want to run the other way from responsibility, when I am most uncertain of my capacity to handle a situation, help me stand firm in Your unfailing grace and blessed assurance. Amen.

Meditation 19

1 Samuel 10:23-27

The narrator speaks: "Then they ran and retrieved Saul from there, and when he stood up in the middle of the people, he was head and shoulders taller than anyone else."

When you are head and shoulders taller than anyone else, don't count on being able to hide in the supplies! His height is pointed out to the people as an indication he is the chosen one, anointed by God to this position. And the people shout: "Long live the king!"

Samuel gives detailed instructions for how this monarchy is to function, the just practices expected of a king, and writes these on a scroll as a legal document. He then sends the people home. In a tidbit of information, the scripture tells us that some courageous men "whose hearts God had touched" go with Saul as he returns home in Gibeah. But others are not impressed with this man anointed by God to be king. One can only imagine the muttering going on: Who does he think he is? My brother would have made a better king than he! For that matter, I would make a better king! Hiding in the supplies, indeed! What sort of king will somebody like that make?

The scripture says they questioned how Saul could possibly save them and they despised him. They didn't bring him gifts, as would have been customary. But Saul does not respond to the denigration, though he surely feels the sting of it. He recognizes the truth they speak about his hiding from his calling, resisting the heavy duty that is now placed upon him.

Sacred Ponderings
When people have been critical of me, perhaps even rightly so, how often have I leaned into my faith, allowed it to sustain me, strengthen me to own up if I have erred, and move on?

Prayerful Pause
Thank you for the strength to move forward even in the face of obstacles.
Amen.

Meditation 20

1 Samuel 11:1-13

The narrator speaks: "Nahash the Ammonite king had been severely oppressing the Gadites and the Reubenites. He gouged out everyone's right eye, thereby not allowing Israel to have a deliverer."

Despite his lackluster initiation as Israel's first king, we quickly see Saul assume leadership in a rather ugly conflict with the Ammonites. As the situation escalates, Saul "burns with anger." It has likely been no small task and an ongoing challenge to take these loosely associated tribes and bring them into some kind of unity. But Saul is so angry he cuts two oxen into pieces and sends them by messengers throughout Israel with an ominous warning: "This is exactly what will be done to the oxen of anyone who doesn't come to the aid of Saul and Samuel!"

Well, this gets their attention! "Great fear of the Lord came over the people, and they came to Saul completely unified." Saul organizes the troops and they successfully attack the Ammonite camp, leaving the few survivors to scatter.

Some of the Israelites now want to execute the people who formerly questioned Saul. But Saul said "No one will be executed because today the Lord has saved Israel."

Sacred Ponderings

The urge for revenge isn't always easy to quell. And, as variously has been quoted, resentment is like drinking poison and hoping it will kill your enemies.

Prayerful Pause

May I resist the urge to act in vengeful ways, O God, and may I instead "heap coals of kindness" on the heads of those I otherwise might be inclined to mistreat.

Meditation 21

1 Samuel 11:14–12:24

Samuel speaks: "Let's go to Gilgal and renew the monarchy there."

Everyone follows Samuel's command to go to Gilgal. There they make Saul king "in the Lord's presence." They offer sacrifices and hold a great celebration. They have much to celebrate! They have vanquished the Ammonites, who created so much fear and destruction. And they have come together under the leadership of Saul, who is now officially recognized as king.

This event creates the opportunity for Samuel to transfer leadership. In a recitation of the ways he has carried out his role as leader, he gives formal recognition to the end of his responsibilities and honors the kingship to which Saul has been ordained.

In what is likely a difficult speech, Samuel entreats the Israelites: "If you will fear the Lord, worship him, obey him, and not rebel against the Lord's command and if both you and the king who rules over you follow the Lord your God—all will be well…Serve the Lord with all your heart."

Sacred Ponderings
What do I hear in Samuel's message that might have meaning for me in my life at this time?

Prayerful Pause
O God, truly may I serve You with all my heart. Amen.

Meditation 22

1 Samuel 13:1-14

The narrator speaks: "Saul was 30 years old when he became king, and he ruled over Israel forty-two years."

We can surmise Saul is likely older than 30 at this point as the scripture immediately follows with his going to war accompanied by his grown son Jonathan. And the number of years he reigns is not certain. But those details aside, what we glean from this passage is much more important: Saul does not obey Samuel's instructions from the Lord and Samuel declares that the Lord "would have established your rule over Israel forever, but now your rule won't last."

Perhaps we would choose as Saul did. As battle preparations mount, the Israelites see they are in trouble: The Philistines have brought "thirty thousand chariots with them, six thousand cavalry, and as many soldiers as there is sand on the seashore to fight Israel." As many soldiers as there is sand on the seashore? The Israelites seek cover! The troops follow Saul to Gilgal where they are to wait for seven days for Samuel. But Samuel does not come when expected. Saul, seeing his troops are beginning to lose faith and desert him, decides to go ahead to offer burnt offerings to the Lord to seek God's favor in battle.

Saul is surely stunned when he goes to welcome Samuel and is greeted with the words "What have you done?...The Lord will search for a man following the Lord's own heart, and the Lord will commission him as leader over God's people, because you didn't keep the Lord's command."

Sacred Ponderings
When have I been castigated for taking an action which seemed to me to be the right thing to do? How did I handle it? What did I learn from it?

Prayerful Pause
God, help me to be faithful, to listen for your leading, to trust You in troubled times, that I may better understand when to wait and what action is called for when the time is right. Amen.

Meditation 23

1 Samuel 14:1-23

Jonathan speaks to his armor-bearer: "Come on! Let's go over to the Philistine fort on the opposite side."

Unlike his father Saul, Jonathan is portrayed as very bold. "Come on, let's go over to the fort of these uncircumcised men," he tells the armor-bearer. "Maybe the Lord will act on our behalf. After all, nothing can stop the Lord from saving, whether there are many soldiers or few." Jonathan relays a plan to the armor-bearer whereby they will know whether the Lord intends for them to engage the Philistines. When the Philistines say "Come on up! We'll teach you a lesson!" Jonathan tells the armor-bearer "Follow me, because the Lord has handed them over to Israel!" Panic breaks out in the camp and this is understood as a terror delivered from God.

Meanwhile, Saul's scouts recognize something going on and report to him the confusion in the Philistine camp. Saul, perhaps still smarting from being denounced by Samuel for acting too quickly, calls on the priest to bring out the Urim and Thummim, the sacred lots thrown to determine whether God's favor is with them.

Saul and his troops enter the battle and prevail and the Lord is given credit for saving Israel that day. Whether this victory enhances Saul's confidence and judgement is the question.

Sacred Ponderings
How do I deal with a lack of confidence? What is my process when faced with a decision? On what are my judgements based?

Prayerful Pause
O God, may I open myself to Your wisdom and grow in the confidence which comes from relationship with You. Amen.

Meditation 24

1 Samuel 14:24-35

The narrator speaks: "Now the Israelite soldiers were in a difficult situation that day because Saul had bound the troops by a solemn pledge: 'Anyone who eats anything before evening when I have taken revenge on my enemies is doomed.'"

What was Saul thinking?? He was travelling with famished troops. Even when they find honeycomb that would have provided some nourishment and instant energy they refuse to eat it. Well, that is, except for Jonathan who somehow had not gotten the word. Only after he had eaten some did someone speak up to say Saul had forbidden this. Jonathan's response is perhaps a mixture of astonishment and disgust: "My father has brought trouble to the land."

Sure enough, at the end of the day, the troops are completely exhausted. So they tear into the plunder of sheep and cattle, eating the meat raw, totally against what they understand to be God's law. When this is reported to Saul, he is furious: "All of you are traitors! Roll a large stone over here right now. Go among the troops and say to them 'Everyone must bring their ox or sheep, and slaughter them here with me. Don't sin against the Lord by eating meat with blood still in it." So they bring the animals to him and Saul builds his first altar to the Lord.

There is a certain rhythm to be established in leadership but Saul seems to be struggling to find it.

Sacred Ponderings
How would I describe my life's rhythm at this time?

Prayerful Pause
O God, I long for the rhythm of my life to be in sync with Your Spirit. Amen.

Meditation 25

1 Samuel 14:36-46

Saul speaks: "Let's go after the Philistines tonight and plunder them until morning. We won't leave them a single survivor."

It seems once again that Saul is trying to correct a previous mistake…… with yet another mistake. His troops were less effective in battle because they were so hungry they couldn't function at peak performance. So now Saul wants to go and "finish the job." But the priest intervenes to say "Let's ask God first." Fortunately, Saul is willing to listen to the priest and asks God "Should I go after the Philistines? Will you hand them over to me?"

When God doesn't answer that day, Saul assumes that there has been some sin committed and says when it is determined who sinned—even if it is his own son Jonathan—that person will be executed. Once again, the sacred lots Urim and Thummin are used. The troops are cleared, leaving only Saul and Jonathan as possible "culprits." Of that draw, Jonathan is shown to be the offending party. Jonathan admits he ate a small bit of honey from the comb the troops had come upon. He protests that it is a small offense to warrant death. But Saul stubbornly insists Jonathan must die. In a rather astonishing twist to this story, the troops adamantly oppose this action, saying that because Jonathan led such a great victory for Israel this day he should be spared because he did so with God's help. At this point, Saul desists. He does not execute Jonathan and he stops chasing the Philistines, who return to their own country.

Sacred Ponderings
Perhaps the Israelites' understanding of God's directing them to fight and causing their victories, as well as their use of drawing on sacred lots to determine such things, seems inscrutable. But when have I perhaps, by intention or error, interpreted my own desires/plans to be those of God?

Prayerful Pause
Influence my desires and plans, O God, and shape my heart to match Your own. Amen.

Meditation 26

1 Samuel 15:1-35

Samuel speaks to Saul: "The Lord sent me to anoint you king over his people Israel. Listen now to the Lord's words! This is what the Lord of heavenly forces says: I am going to punish the Amalekites for what they did to Israel: how they attacked the Israelites as they came up from Egypt. So go! Attack the Amalekites; put everything that belongs to them under the ban. Spare no one. Kill men and women, children and infants, oxen and sheep, camels and donkeys."

While some still might espouse such extreme measures, to most of our ears this sounds abominable, particularly because it purports to come from a loving God. But the message that was perhaps more likely heard then and is certainly one for us to hear now, is about obedience, our lives as "living sacrifices."

Saul and his troops keep the best animals and everything else of value for themselves and Saul takes King Agag captive. When Samuel arrives and confronts him with "What is this noise I hear?" (i.e. the bleating of the animals that were spared), Saul says they only kept them to sacrifice them to the Lord. Samuel reminds Saul that he was appointed king over Israel, and that he had been given instructions in that role by God…instructions not followed. When Saul protests, Samuel declares, "Does the Lord want entirely burned offerings and sacrifices as much as obedience to the Lord? Listen to this: obeying is better than sacrificing, paying attention is better than fat from rams."

Saul says he indeed has sinned but claims he was "afraid of the troops and obeyed them." He pleads with Samuel to stay and worship with him. Samuel says no because Saul has rejected the Lord's instructions and now the Lord rejects Saul. Saul entreats Samuel further and ultimately Samuel stays. When Samuel does finally return to his home in Gibeah, however, he continues to grieve over Saul, and we are told God regrets having made Saul the king.

Sacred Pondering
The only other time in scripture in which we are told God had regrets was just prior to the story of Noah and the flood, when he was grieved over the people he had created and the way they were living their lives. What do I see in my own life or witness in the world today that might inspire God's "grief"?

Prayerful Pause
May the life I offer God be living prayer, living sacrifice, a reflection of God in the world around me.

Meditation 27

1 Samuel 16:1-13

The Lord speaks: "How long are you going to grieve over Saul? I have rejected him as king over Israel. Fill your horn with oil and get going. I'm sending you to Jesse of Bethlehem because I have found my next king among his sons."

These instructions are intimidating to Samuel to say the least. He is certain Saul will kill him if he seeks out the next king. But he listens to the Lord's instructions for how he is to go about this and follows through as indicated.

The scriptures are fascinating in the repetition of this theme: God seeks out the lowliest, the most unlikely. When Samuel is struck by the appearance of Eliab and assumes he must be the chosen one, the Lord tells him, "Have no regard for his appearance or stature…….God doesn't look at things like humans do. Humans see only what is visible to the eyes, but the Lord sees into the heart." Jesse presents more of his sons in order. None of these are selected by the Lord. Samuel, likely puzzled, asks "Is that all of your boys?" Well, in fact, there is one more, the youngest, David, who is out tending sheep. Who would consider him, the youngest, engaged in the commonplace work as sheepherder, a likely candidate for the role of king? Apparently, the Lord does! And Samuel anoints him before his brothers and the scriptures report that "The Lord's spirit came over David from that point forward."

Sacred Ponderings
How often do we overlook folks, perhaps the waitress who brings our order or the homeless man sitting outside the restaurant? The cashier at the grocery store or the person behind us in line?

Prayerful Pause
O God, open my eyes that I may see.

Meditation 28

1 Samuel 16:14-23

The narrator speaks: "Now the Lord's spirit had departed from Saul, and an evil spirit from the Lord tormented him."

Given some of the descriptions of Saul's behavior when overtaken by what scriptures describe as an evil spirit, it is no wonder the servants consider looking for some way to soothe him. No one wants to be in that line of fire! The benefits of music having long been recognized, they seek out a musician. And who might that be? Our young sheep herder shows up for duty! He comes with quite a reference: a good musician…a strong man…heroic…a warrior who speaks well…good looking…the Lord is with him. We have not only a solution for the current problem of Saul's violent moods but a foretelling of David's place in the future of Israel.

Saul immediately takes to David and requests that he be permanently in Saul's service as armor-bearer. Scriptures report David is quite effective in calming Saul with the music of his lyre…at least for the present moment.

Sacred Ponderings
What gifts might I have to offer comfort to others? Am I willing to "show up" when opportunities present themselves?

Prayerful Pause
May I recognize my gifts and willingly offer them when You open the way for me to do so.

Meditation 29

1 Samuel 17:1-58

The narrator speaks: "A champion named Goliath from Gath came out from the Philistine camp. He was more than nine feet tall…His spear shaft was as strong as the bar on a weaver's loom, and its iron head weighed fifteen pounds."

When not actively engaged in battle with the Philistines, the Israelites seem always to be on the verge of it. In this passage we have the challenge of Goliath and the description of David's mighty deed following his anointing and his receiving of God's Spirit.

Goliath, nine feet tall and clad in armor and well equipped with weapons, issues the challenge that if anyone can kill him, the Philistines will become the servants of Israel. "For forty days straight" (i.e. for a very long time in Biblical terminology) "the Philistine came out and took his stand both morning and evening." David is still tending sheep, but going back and forth between sheepherding and taking supplies to his brothers who serve in the army. When he hears of this challenge, he is incensed that Goliath is getting away with "insulting the army of the living God." His brothers are annoyed with him, because he is not with the sheep. Indeed, scripture reports Eliab saying "I know how arrogant you are and your devious plan: you came down just to see the battle!"

When Saul hears that David has in fact offered to go against the Philistine, he sends for him but is skeptical that David is equipped to do this. David is adamant that he can do it because he has killed lions and bears who have threatened the flock. He is permitted to respond to the challenge and famously says to Goliath: "You are coming against me with sword, spear and scimitar, but I come against you in the name of the Lord of heavenly forces, the God of Israel's army, the one you've insulted. Today the Lord will hand you over to me." David, without so much as a sword, fells the giant with a simple stone. And the Philistines, predictably, flee.

Sacred Ponderings
David projected great confidence as he took on a formidable task. Am I feeling overwhelmed by anything facing me at this time? How might I respond?

Prayerful Pause
Where I lack confidence, may I trust Your Spirit to guide me and bless my efforts, whatever the outcome.

Meditation 30

1 Samuel 18:1-30

The women from all of Israel's towns sing: "Saul has killed his thousands, but David has killed his tens of thousands."

Trouble is on the horizon now! Saul burns with anger when he feels he is being humiliated by David's success. Saul begins to monitor David, fearing he is after the kingdom. Saul's mood turns ugly and David attempts to calm him with the lyre. But, instead, Saul takes his spear and hurls it towards David!

Matters only become worse. "Everyone in Israel and Judah loved David because he led them out in war and back again." So Saul sends David into battle hoping that the Philistines will kill him. Not so! Then, in a curious twist, Saul encourages David to marry into the family. When he initially refuses, Saul later tries again, offering his younger daughter Michal, who loves David. In Saul's twisted thinking, "I'll give her to him…she'll cause him problems, and the Philistines will be against him."

He instructs his servants to suggest to David that the king likes him and the servants love him and he really should become the king's son in law.

This plan backfires on Saul. "When Saul knew for certain that the Lord was with David and that his daughter Michal loved him, then Saul was even more afraid of David. Saul was David's enemy for the rest of his life. And whenever the Philistine commanders came out for battle, David would have more success than the rest of Saul's officers, so his fame spread widely."

Sacred Ponderings
When has jealousy gotten the best of me? What was the outcome? How do I understand this aspect of myself and how do I handle it?

Prayerful Pause
When I fall prey to jealousy, O God, turn my heart instead towards love and greater understanding of myself and others.

Epilogue

1 Samuel 19: 1-24

Jonathan speaks: "The king shouldn't do anything wrong to his servant David, because he hasn't wronged you. In fact, his actions have helped you greatly. He risked his own life when he killed that Philistine, and the Lord won a great victory for all Israel. You saw it and were happy about it. Why then would you do something wrong to an innocent person by killing David for no reason"

Saul's son Jonathan, who is the beloved friend of David, acts on David's behalf numerous times in attempts to spare his life from Saul. Even David's wife Michal had to intervene once, tricking Saul's servants into believing David was ill while she arranged his escape. When Saul's messengers are sent to track David down to kill him, they encounter a group of prophets in a prophetic frenzy, with Samuel leading them. The messengers also are overcome with this frenzy. Then Saul himself comes and, reminiscent of his experience when he was first anointed by Samuel, the Spirit of God comes over him as well. He takes off all his clothes before Samuel and lays naked "that whole day and night."

It would seem Saul's earlier experience of his anointing resurfaces at this critical juncture, sparing David, the one who has more recently become God's anointed. This left people wondering: "Is Saul also one of the prophets?"

Sacred Ponderings
Has something been re-awakened in me? Am I alert for and open to God's Presence?

Prayerful Pause
Dear God, when I am at my worst, re-awaken Your Spirit in me, help me to reclaim Your Presence in my life. Amen.

Our Story Continues

God's Truth Surfaces in Human Tales

In the first six chapters of Daniel we have folktales of young Jewish men working during exile in Babylon, describing Daniel's faithfulness to God when such behavior risked clear and present danger to himself. In contrast, we have the parable of Jonah, where Jonah resists faithfulness to God's call. Might we recognize in these stories how we can desire and dare to follow God…and yet sometimes be met by our own resistance?

Meditation 1

Daniel 1:1-7

In 606 or 605 BCE, Babylon defeated Egypt and became a superpower in the Near East. Actually, Nebuchadnezzar wasn't yet king at the time of this verse, and evidence is lacking that he attacked Jerusalem this early. Possibly incorrect historical information is deliberate by the storytellers in an effort to convey to the listeners that this is intended to be fiction. In any case, we have the entrance of Daniel and his three companions Hananiah, Mishael, and Azariah into the court by virtue of King Nebuchadnezzar's search for "good-looking young men without defects, skilled in all wisdom, possessing knowledge, conversant with learning and capable of serving in the king's palace."

The four are to be taught the Chaldean (Babylonian) language and its literature and to be fed from the king's own food and royal wine. This is no small thing to be eating the king's food and drinking his wine. This is not meant as a kind gesture towards the young men. It indicates a symbol of loyalty to and fellowship with the king. The expectations of these selected Jews are enormous! And given the importance of names in ancient times, the king gives them new ones, names which reflect the names of gods in the Babylonian culture. Daniel becomes Belteshazzar—Bel being the title of Marduk, god of Babylon—and his friends are now called by Shadrach, Meshach and Abednego, names perhaps connected to the gods Nabu and Aku. What is this foursome in for?!

Sacred Ponderings
Have I ever been attracted to a glittering opportunity or found myself in a puzzling situation only to discover that the cost of my involvement was too dear?

Prayerful Pause
God help me to discern my responsibility to myself and others in life's encounters and to remain faithful to You.

Meditation 2

Daniel 1:8-17

Yikes! Already Daniel and his friends are encountering the king's expectations of them head on. Daniel has decided that he won't "pollute himself with the king's rations or the royal wine." The scripture doesn't indicate he struggles with this decision. The story is designed to point towards Daniel's faithfulness. But we might surmise that someone in this position would not make such a decision without counting the cost. This is quite an awakening to realize that the great benefits to serving in the palace mean being subservient not only to the king's wishes to have them trained to serve in the king's court. They are expected to totally give their lives over to the culture.

Daniel has a good relationship with the chief official and relays his intention not to partake. As one might imagine, the official is frightened by such a choice because he fears his own life will be the target of the king's wrath. Daniel has an ingenious solution! "Why not test your servants for ten days? You could give us a diet of vegetables to eat and water to drink. Then compare our appearance to the appearance of the young men who eat the king's food. Then deal with your servants according to what you see." And it works in an astonishing way: not only are they healthier but God gives "knowledge, mastery of all literature, and wisdom to these four men." And Daniel himself gains "understanding of every type of vision and dream."

Sacred Ponderings
When have I taken time lately to marvel at my own God-given ability to think through a problem or to fathom God's working in my life in totally unexpected ways?

Prayerful Pause
Dear God, help me to pay attention to my life! Amen.

Meditation 3

Daniel 2:1-13

Dreams being highly valued in the ancient world for whatever information might be gleaned from them leads kings to seek out those who can interpret them. In the second year of King Nebuchadnezzar's reign he begins to have very disturbing dreams. Anxiously he calls for "the dream interpreters, enchanters, diviners, and Chaldeans" to explain his dreams to him. However, he apparently expects them to be able to determine the dreams without his actually telling them the content. When they offer to expound upon their meaning once the king has revealed the dream itself, Nebuchadnezzar accuses them of stalling for time. They protest that this is impossible: "No king or ruler, no matter how great, has ever asked such a thing of any dream interpreter, enchanter, or Chaldean…No one could declare the dream to the king but the gods, who don't live among mere humans."

More often than not kings in the Old Testament are portrayed as short on anger management skills! Nebuchadnezzar is in a rage now and orders all Babylon's sages be executed—to include Daniel and his friends! Imagine the chaos in the court…terrified "dream interpreters, enchanters, diviners, and Chaldeans" being rounded up…people scurrying around the king trying to calm him down. What wisdom will be called forth in Daniel now?

Sacred Ponderings
When chaos ensues around me, what is my response? How might I stay centered? What wisdom might I draw on?

Prayerful Ponderings
In what time I am afraid, O God, may I trust in You.

Meditation 4

Daniel 2:14-45

Once again Daniel comes through in a crisis! Into the chaos, Daniel, using "wisdom and sound judgment," investigates what all the commotion is about, dares to go directly to the king to suggest Nebuchadnezzar allow him some time to consider this. The king, apparently more willing to listen to reason at this point, permits Daniel to do so. Daniel then goes to his companions and relays the situation to them. They pray for God's guidance, with the result that the mystery is revealed to Daniel. Daniel presses Arioch, the one appointed to kill all the sages, not to follow through with the executions. Then he proceeds to approach King Nebuchadnezzar.

As we might well expect, Daniel assures the king he can both report and interpret the dream not because of his own powers but because of the power coming from "a God in heaven, a revealer of mysteries." Daniel describes that the huge statue that was smashed in the king's dream hints at another kingdom that will supplant Nebuchadnezzar's, actually a succession of kingdoms (foreshadowing the apocalyptic writings in the second half of Daniel). "But in the days of those kings, the God of heaven will raise up an everlasting kingdom that will be indestructible. Its rule will never pass to another people. It will shatter other kingdoms. It will put an end to all of them. It will stand firm forever."

Sacred Ponderings
Daniel doesn't act on impulse, doesn't rush to the king's quarters nor does he retreat out of fear. But he does go about the process thoughtfully and doesn't shrink back from addressing the king directly.

How thoughtfully do I consider difficult situations? Am I more likely to be impulsive or more inclined to be risk averse? Am I willing to "address the king directly" when a problem occurs?

Prayerful Pause
May I be willing to model Daniel's behavior, to thoughtfully approach problems and to respectfully address directly the people involved. Amen.

Meditation 5

Daniel 2:46–3:7

Amazing! King Nebuchadnezzar bows low and honors Daniel! How often have they seen their king do this?! "No doubt about it," Nebuchadnezzar says, "your God is God of gods, Lord of kings, and a revealer of mysteries because you were able to reveal this mystery!" But he no sooner says that before he turns around and makes a gold statue, purportedly ninety feet high and nine feet wide. We have a bit of tongue in cheek in this story as the writer pokes some fun at the over-sized egos of rulers. Repeatedly the writer takes us through the list of the many officials and the extravagance of their ceremony: "King Nebuchadnezzar then ordered the chief administrators, ministers, governors, counselors, treasurers, judges, magistrates, and all the provincial officials to assemble and come for the dedication of the statue that he had set up. So the chief administrators, ministers, governors, counselors, treasurers, judges, magistrates, and all the provincial officials assembled for the dedication of the statue that King Nebuchadnezzar had set up."

The herald proclaims loudly: "People, nations, and languages! This is what you must do: When you hear the sound of the horn, pipe, zither, lyre, harp, flute, and every kind of instrument, you must bow down and worship the gold statue that King Nebuchadnezzar has set up. Anyone who will not bow down and worship will be immediately thrown into a furnace of flaming fire." It isn't rocket science, as we say, to figure out what this means for Daniel and his friends!

Sacred Ponderings
Like the writer of Daniel, we may often make fun of or complain about government or our bosses or others in some sort of authority. But are we often among the "people, nations, and languages" who choose to "go along to get along"? How do we begin to influence systems which we recognize are in need of change?

Prayerful Pause
I pray for wisdom, O God, to know when and how to intervene in those times when the situation calls for (sometimes screams out for!) change.

Meditation 6

Daniel 3:8-18

Well, wouldn't you just know it: some of the Chaldeans see their opportunity to put these "uppity" Jews "in their place," even into the path of what would seem to be certain death. Just listen to their contrived little speech to the king: "Long live the king! Your Majesty, you gave a command that everyone who hears the sound of the horn, pipe, zither, lyre, harp, flute, and every kind of instrument should bow down and worship the gold statue. Anyone who wouldn't bow and worship would be thrown into a furnace of flaming fire. Now there are some Jews, ones you appointed (these Chaldeans take pains to mention!) to administer the province of Babylon—specifically, Shadrach, Meshach, and Abednego—who have ignored your command. They don't serve your gods, and they don't worship the gold statue you've set up."

Well, of course, given what we know about Nebuchadnezzar, this is all it takes to send him into a violent rage. Nebuchadnezzar orders them brought before him and gives them one more chance to bow down to the statue or be thrown in the fire. He taunts them a little: "Then what god will rescue you from my power?"

But Shadrach, Meshach, and Abednego stand firm: "If our God—the one we serve—is able to rescue us from the furnace of flaming fire and from your power, Your Majesty, then let him rescue us. But if he doesn't, know this for certain, Your Majesty: we will never serve your gods or worship the gold statue you've set up."

Sacred Ponderings
What chutzpah! They are unfailingly respectful even as they most adamantly disobey the king!

Prayerful Pause
May I be more like Shadrach, Meshach and Abednego and less like the Chaldeans or Nebuchadnezzar.

Meditation 7

Daniel 3:19-27

Oh, now King Nebuchadnezzar is so angry his face is "twisted beyond recognition!" His voice is likely so shrill it is hardly recognizable when he orders that the furnace be heated to seven times its normal heat. The unfortunate men who carry out that command are burned up themselves because of the extreme intensity of the fire.

We have no evidence Nebuchadnezzar is at all fazed by the loss of these men but his attention is definitely captured when he counts four figures in the flames where three were thrown: "Didn't we throw three men, bound, into the fire?" he asks, shocked. They assure him it was only three: "Look!" he exclaims, "I see four men, unbound, walking around inside the fire, and they aren't hurt! And the fourth one looks like one of the gods." He calls Shadrach, Meshach, and Abednego to come out of the fire, calling them "servants of the Most High God." Everyone crowds around to witness this enigma. The men have been totally unaffected by the flames: their hair is not singed, their clothes look as before and do not even smell of smoke!

Sacred Ponderings
Nebuchadnezzar might have considered the testimony of faith in their God as a miracle in itself, given the king's propensity for reckless behavior and his exaggerated sense of power. Instead it takes a miracle so dramatic that it is impossible for him to dismiss.

Prayerful Pause
O God, I pray to appreciate the miracles that abound around me. Amen.

Meditation 8

Daniel 3:28–4:3

Ever mercurial, Nebuchadnezzar declares that the God of Shadrach, Meshach, and Abednego be praised. He recounts the story of their refusal to follow the king's orders to worship the statue and their willingness to sacrifice their very bodies if necessary in order to remain faithful to their God. But somehow he misses the very essence of what it means to live in such a relationship with one's God because in his very next breath he decrees that "whoever speaks disrespectfully about Shadrach, Meshach, and Abednego's God will be torn limb from limb and their house made a trash heap, because there is no other god who can rescue like this."

Magnanimously, Nebuchadnezzar greets "all the peoples, nations, and languages inhabiting the entire earth" with the message "I wish you much peace." He continues to witness to God's mystery and majesty: "His signs are superb! His miracles so powerful! His kingdom is everlasting. His rule is for all time." So that is what he is saying for the moment. Can his subjects dare trust this?

Sacred Pause
Contrast the more understated way Shadrach, Meshach and Abednego convey their faith and the more exaggerated way Nebuchadnezzar goes about testifying to God's mighty works in his life.

Prayerful Pause
May my faith be integrated into every aspect of my life so that when I speak people recognize authenticity.

Meditation 9

Daniel 4:4-8

Once again King Nebuchadnezzar is dreaming! And also once again, he first orders all Babylon's sages to come before him. One wonders what the life of a sage was like in that era. You are at the king's beck and call. The potential for an order to appear before the king must provide an ongoing stressor as your fate seems to hang in the balance between your ability to provide him credible interpretation and the king's ability to bring your life to a nasty conclusion if he isn't pleased.

And what about Daniel? Why is he not the first to be called on, given his history with the king? Daniel, who interpreted his dreams before and gave the credit to God, to whom Nebuchadnezzar then offered effusive praise? "Daniel, who is called Belteshazzar after the name of my god, was the last to come before me," he says and then declares, "In him is the breath of the holy gods!" So he hasn't forgotten his previous experience with Daniel. And we surmise the story is told in this way to emphasize again that Daniel through God's power could do what all the other sages could not. The writer wants to remind us that God's power is always greater than the circumstances might suggest!

Sacred Ponderings
There is notable difference between the anxiety of the sages and the confidence of Daniel. When does anxiety get the best of me? What is different about those times when I am more confident?

Prayerful Pause
O God, help me always to remember Your power is always greater than my circumstances might indicate! Amen

Meditation 10

Daniel 4:9-18

Nebuchadnezzar, perhaps more trusting now of Daniel, does not require Daniel to know what the dream is without Nebuchadnezzar's telling him. Instead he describes a dream of a tree, growing in size and strength, high as the sky, visible from every corner of the earth. "Its leaves were beautiful, its fruit abundant; it had enough food for everyone. Wild animals took shade under it; birds nested in its branches. All living things lived off that tree." Well, that doesn't seem so disturbing…but then he dreams that a "holy watcher came down from heaven. He proclaimed loudly: 'Cut down the tree and shear off its branches."

The tree, a symbol recognized in myths and dreams around the world as a metaphor for order and power, takes on great meaning here. Nebuchadnezzar's power is threatened and beyond that there is prediction that Nebuchadnezzar will go through a lengthy period of insanity. However, the trees deepest roots will be left in the earth, bound with iron and bronze.

"This sentence," as Nebuchadnezzar continues to describe the experience of the dream, "is by the watcher's decree; this decision is the holy one's word so that all who live might know that the Most High dominates human kingship." We have some sense that Nebuchadnezzar's inflated sense of importance and power is about to be tested.

Sacred Ponderings
Consider "the trees deepest roots will be left in the earth, bound with iron and bronze." What grounds me in the midst of my deepest fears?

Prayerful Pause
Send my roots deeper into Your Spirit and bind me with the iron of Your grace and the bronze of Your love. Amen.

Meditation 11

Daniel 4:19-27

Daniel is "shocked for a bit" the scriptures tell us. And who wouldn't be? Things had seemed to be going well enough. In an interesting reversal, and perhaps an indication of a growing relationship with Daniel, the king says "Don't let the dream and its interpretation scare you, Belteshazzar." Daniel wisely prefaces his interpretation to the king with the words "Sir, I wish the dream to be for those who hate you and its meaning be for your enemies." He proceeds to tell Nebuchadnezzar that the tree represents the king, who has grown large and become powerful. But the dream means that it is "the sentence of the Most High" that the king will be driven away from other humans and will live with the wild animals, eat grass like cattle. "Seven periods of time will pass over you, until you acknowledge that the Most High dominates human kingship, giving it to anyone he wants…the kingship will again be yours, once you acknowledge that heaven rules all. Therefore, Your Majesty, please accept my advice: remove your sins by doing what is right: remove your wrongdoing by showing mercy to the poor. Then your safety will be long lasting."

What a meaty passage this is! God is not impressed with King Nebuchadnezzar's importance and power but expects Nebuchadnezzar to come to terms with the fact that all that he is and has comes from a Source greater than himself.

Sacred Ponderings
What message might I recognize for myself in this story? What wrongdoing do I recognize that needs correction? When have I shown mercy lately?

Prayerful Pause
May I be always aware of the Source greater than myself. Amen.

Meditation 12

Daniel 4:28-33

King Nebuchadnezzar, as are we all, is subject to denial. Despite this astounding and surely distressing message he has just received, for twelve months he continues on the same path, taking pride in his kingdom and his perceived accomplishments. Walking on the roof of his royal palace all these months later, he declares: "Isn't this Babylon, the magnificent city that I built as the royal house by my own mighty strength and for my own majestic glory?" (Really? HE built the magnificent city all by himself? Hardly!) Scripture tells us the words "hadn't even left the king's mouth when a voice came from heaven: 'You, King Nebuchadnezzar, are now informed: Kingship is taken away from you. You will be driven away from other humans and will live with the wild animals. You will eat grass like cattle, and seven periods of time will pass over you until you acknowledge that the Most High dominates human kingship, giving it to anyone he wants.'"

As we often discover, there are a lot of what might be considered interesting details missing from these verses. We are told the sentence is immediately carried out and that he was driven away. Carried out by whom? Who drew the short straw for that assignment? "Driven away" implies Nebuchadnezzar didn't just willingly comply with this sentence he had known but denied was inevitable. But the point is clearly made that taking credit for whatever success one has without acknowledging all the people who contributed to it and the God whose Spirit sustains you, has consequences that will catch up to you.

Sacred Ponderings
When does my own denial blind me to realities to which I best give my attention? When might I have failed to give credit where credit was due?

Prayerful Pause
God, may I have eyes to see truth and a heart willing to acknowledge the many and the One who have made my accomplishments possible.

Meditation 13

Daniel 4:34-37

At long last, Nebuchadnezzar comes to his senses. He recounts: "My reason returned to me, and I praised the Most High. I worshipped and glorified the one who lives forever because his rule is everlasting; his kingdom is for all time. All of earth's inhabitants are nothing in comparison. The Most High does whatever he wants with heaven's forces and with earth's inhabitants. No one can contain his power or say to him, 'What do you think you are doing?'"

It is at this point that Nebuchadnezzar says he was returned to his right mind. Everything is returned in fact. He regains his honor and splendor. His associates and princes once again want to be with him. And he is even more successful than before. He reiterates that "Now I, Nebuchadnezzar, worship, magnify, and glorify the king of heaven. All his works are truth, all his paths are justice, and he is able to humble all who walk in pride."

For those who have gone through a really dark time in their lives, this sudden return to mental, physical and spiritual health may seem disingenuous. Digging our way out of those periods can be an erratic process and the results are not always as dramatic as this. But that is not the writer's emphasis. We are to understand what is punctuated: All God's works are truth, all God's paths are justice, and God is able to humble all who walk in pride.

Sacred Ponderings
King Nebuchadnezzar's lack of humility mirrors what we can see in our world—and sometimes in ourselves.

Prayerful Pause
O, God, may I renounce hubris and embrace humility. Amen.

Meditation 14

Daniel 5:1-4

Nebuchadnezzar, the feared and accomplished king, has passed on. Belshazzar, the last Babylonian king, now rules. But he is less of a serious figure, more of what might be termed "party animal." He throws a huge party for "a thousand of his princes." While under the influence of a significant amount of alcohol, he commands that "the gold and silver equipment that his father Nebuchadnezzar had taken from Jerusalem's temple be brought to the party so that the king, his princes, his consorts, and his secondary wives could drink out of them."

One might surmise, given King Nebuchadnezzar's experience, that these goblets were recognized as sacred, were securely stored and likely never used. But Belshazzar appears only to be intent on livening up the party a bit. "So the gold equipment that had been carried out of the temple, God's house in Jerusalem, was brought in; and the king, his princes, his consorts, and his secondary wives drank out of it."

Does no one raise objection? Apparently not. Not only do they all drink a lot of wine out of these sacred containers but, to add insult to injury, they praise not the Most High, but "the gods of gold, silver, bronze, wood and stone."

Sacred Ponderings
"Slaps in the face" to God, devaluing the sacred, can take many forms. Our neighbors are sacred. Earth and air and water are sacred, entrusted to our care. Before we are incensed by Belshazzar's and his company's behavior, let us consider our own disregard for the sacred.

Prayerful Pause
Give me grace, I pray, to recognize the sacred all around me and to own my responsibility towards my neighbors and all Your creation.

Meditation 15

Daniel 5:5-9

Belshazzar is about to get his comeuppance. Suddenly, in the soft glow of the wall sconce and in the midst of the "afterglow" of so much wine, fingers of a human hand appear on the plaster of the palace wall. Belshazzar's vision is perhaps blurred a bit from the alcohol. But he sees "the writing on the wall." The party comes to an abrupt halt.

"The king's mood changed immediately, and he was deeply disturbed. He felt weak, and his knees were shaking." The enchanters and the Chaldeans and the diviners once again are called into service. What a daunting task! Dreams are difficult enough. But who before has seen handwriting on the wall? So they are, predictably, totally stumped, leaving the king even more frightened than before. Perhaps despite the fuzzy state of his brain he begins to review his behavior over the course of the night, or perhaps over the course of his reign.

Belshazzar and likely all who participated are having serious regrets, "buyer's remorse" as it were, after buying an evening of indulgence with no thought given to paying the consequences.

Sacred Ponderings
Sometimes what seems like a small indiscretion, a minor misstep escalates into something we would have never expected, predicted. A little forethought would have gone a long way in mitigating this disaster.

Prayerful Pause
When I am inclined to ignore Your Still Small Voice that I am veering off the path, help me, O God, to stop and to listen… and to act accordingly. Amen.

Meditation 16

Daniel 5:10-12

Remember this was no intimate little dinner party. There were a thousand princes, consorts and "secondary wives" in attendance. The uproarous party has turned into a melee. Into this chaos the queen comes to wield some influence.

"Long live the king!" she says. "Don't be so disturbed. Don't be so frightened. There is a man in your kingdom who has the breath of holy gods in him! When your father was alive, this man was shown to possess illumination, insight, and wisdom like the very wisdom of the gods."

This is perhaps the king's mother or even grandmother. She certainly has knowledge of Daniel's history in the palace. Daniel is an old man now and his position has likely diminished over the years. But the queen is quite insistent that Daniel is the resource they should be calling on: "Your father King Nebuchadnezzar appointed this man as chief over the dream interpreters, enchanters, Chaldeans, and diviners." Perhaps he questions her. Perhaps he knows of Daniel but considers him a "has been," no longer capable. She continues, "Yes, your father did this because this man—Daniel, the one the king named Belteshazzar—possesses an extraordinary spirit, knowledge, and insight into the meaning of dreams. He can explain ambiguities and resolve mysteries. Now in light of all that, summon Daniel! He will explain the meaning of this thing."

Sacred Ponderings
How easily we sometimes dismiss someone because of age or disability or some perceived lack in skills or capacity.

Prayerful Pause
O God, take off my blinders, strip me of my biased judgements.

Meditation 17

Daniel 5:13-31

Although promised royal robes, a gold chain around his neck and position as third in command in the kingdom, Daniel rejects all these things, tells the king to keep his gifts, give them to someone else. Perhaps there is a weariness in his voice as he says this because he has been through this already multiple times with Belshazzar's father. Perhaps he sighs to himself: Do they never learn?

Nevertheless, he agrees to interpret the handwriting on the wall. He recounts how Nebuchadnezzar became stubborn and arrogant and lost his throne and all his glory because of it. He points out Belshazzar has known that history and ignored it. He reminds Beshazzar how he took the equipment of God's house and drank from it, all the while praising gods "who can't see, hear or know anything. But you didn't glorify the true God who holds your very breath in his hand and who owns every road you take."

So goes Daniel's interpretation: "This is the meaning of the word MENE: God has numbered the days of your rule. It's over! TEKEL means that you've been weighed on the scales, and you don't measure up. PERES means your kingship is divided and given to the Medes and Persians."

Thus Daniel, as promised, despite his declining the honor, is dresed in a purple robe, is decorated with a gold chain around his neck and made third in command in the kingdom…and that very night, Belshazzar is killed and Darius the Mede takes over.

Sacred Ponderings
Poignant messages reside here about willful ignorance, egotism and the impermanence of life.

Prayerful Pause
Forgive me when I choose ignorance over awareness, arrogance over humility and disregard over gratitude.

Meditation 18

Daniel 6:1-9

King Darius, who has now become the king, organizes his administration by appointing 120 chief administrators throughout the kingdom and designates three main officers to whom these administrators report, Daniel among the three. Daniel seems to have regained ground since reading the writing on the wall to Belshazzar. He is recognized for his extraordinary spirit and his work is clearly superior to the other officers. So, in a theme we so often encounter in the scriptures and sometimes in our own experience, his counterparts begin to look for ways to remove him—permanently.

When Daniel's work and personal life is exemplary and there is no flaw to be found, the other officers seek to manipulate the king to mandate that for thirty days anyone who says prayers to any god or human being except the king shall be thrown into a den of lions.

"Now, Your Majesty," they say solicitously, "issue the law and sign the document so that it cannot be changed, as per the law of Media and Persia, which cannot be annulled." (Here the writer pokes some fun at Persia's claim to unassailable laws. History even provides us with the translated inscription on King Darius' grave: "What was said to them by me, that they did; my law—that held them firm.")

Darius, who is easily conned into this and doesn't like to be bothered too much with administration anyway, signs this into law.

Sacred Ponderings
Manipulation can be fairly mild. Even as children we learn certain behaviors may be employed to get our desired end. But when it becomes a pattern of relating or expands into destructive behaviors, we must take heed.

Prayerful Pause
May I be more focused on living in Your Spirit and less intent on getting what I want.

Meditation 19

Daniel 6:10-22

As we might well expect, it takes no time at all for the officers' plan to fall into place. Daniel prays as is his custom. The officers can hardly get to the king's palace fast enough. Breathless, they exclaim, "Your Majesty! Didn't you sign a law, that for thirty days any person who prays to any god or human being besides you, Your Majesty, would be thrown into a pit of lions?" Perhaps absentmindedly the king replies, "The decision is absolutely firm." Like tattletale school children they report, "One of the Judean exiles, Daniel, has ignored you, our Majesty, as well as the law you signed. He says his prayers three times a day!"

In an interesting twist to this story, the king is quite disturbed by this turn of events. The scriptures tell us he did "everything he could do to save Daniel before the sun went down." The king has backed himself into a corner. He signed the law; he loses face if he doesn't uphold his own law. Darius gives the order but before Daniel is hurled into the lions' den, he tells Daniel, "Your God—the one you serve so consistently—will rescue you."

King Darius fasts through the night, unable to sleep. At dawn he wastes no time rushing to the pit where Daniel was thrown. He calls to Daniel, asking if God rescued him. To his relief, Daniel replies, "Long live the king! My God sent his messenger, who shut the lions' mouths. They haven't touched me because I was judged innocent before my God. I haven't done anything to you either, Your Majesty," he adds.

Sacred Ponderings
Psalm 103:4 reads God "saves your life from the pit." What "pit" might I recognize in my own life?

Prayerful Pause
When I encounter places so deep and dark that I feel like I have been thrown into a pit, I pray for grace to be as steadfast as Daniel. Amen.

Meditation 20

Daniel 6:23-28

King Darius, ecstatic at Daniel's survival, commands that he be removed from the pit. Not a scratch is found on him, scripture reveals "because he trusted in his God." We are not necessarily prepared for his next move as he throws the officers who colluded against Daniel—along with their wives and children!—into the pit where they are immediately consumed by the lions. The writer provides this as additional evidence that God spared Daniel from lions who were indeed hungry.

It appears laws can be changed afterall! Darius now issues another decree that "In every region of my kingdom, all people must fear and revere Daniel's God" because:

"He is the living God. God stands firm forever. His kingship is indestructible. God performs signs and miracles in heaven and on earth." He offers as proof of this Daniel's experience in the lions' den.

And the steadfast Daniel is reported to prosper throughout the rule of Darius followed by the rule of Cyrus the Persian.

Sacred Ponderings
Imagine being an Israelite in exile in Babylon hearing this story. How might this have been comprehended in the ancient world?

Prayerful Pause
May I be both firm as Daniel in my conviction of God faithfulness and as flexible as Darius when change is necessary.

We now shift from the folktales of the first half of Daniel and turn to the story of Jonah, a parable-like book. The Common English Bible sheds light on this unusual tale:

"The account of Jonah and his adventures in Nineveh is by far the most peculiar writing in the prophetic literature of the Bible. The story is more about the prophet's actions than his words. The book also focuses on foreigners, non-Israelites, who receive God's mercy, which is surprising in the Old Testament. A reluctant prophet preaches to his enemies, and the Ninevites change their hearts and lives to receive God's mercy…

"This particular story about a prophet named Jonah isn't historical in the narrow sense. Instead readers should receive Jonah as an extended metaphor marked by wordplay, suspense, intra-biblical allusions, satire, irony, hyperbole, and humor. Much like a parable, the book of Jonah teaches that 'deliverance belongs to the Lord' (Jon 2:9), even if that deliverance comes to the most unlikely candidates. Much like a satire, Jonah contains extraordinary events and extravagant characters designed to amuse and delight the reader. Much like a novella, the narrative has a clearly defined hero (God) and a haphazard rival (Jonah)."

Let us proceed to join Jonah in his adventures!

Meditation 21

Jonah 1:1-3

We don't know what Jonah is doing when the Lord's word comes to him. Maybe he is just waking up after a restless sleep. Maybe he is busy contemplating his next prophecy. Maybe he is relaxing a bit before turning in for the night. Whatever he is up to, there seems to be no ignoring the Lord's voice: "Get up and go to Nineveh, that great city, and cry out against it, for their evil has come to my attention."

Well, Jonah jumps up and packs his bag…and heads the opposite direction! He is going to flee to Tarshish to avoid the Lord. He goes to Joppa and there he seeks out a ship headed for Tarshish. He doesn't even seem to have second thoughts. Nope, he pays the fare and boards the ship.

He probably looks like any other passenger, although it is worth speculating that someone fleeing from the Lord might look suspiciously nervous. Maybe someone notices him and wonders to himself, What's his problem?

Sacred Ponderings
Do I recognize anything in myself that is resistant to listening for and responding to those things I understand God to be calling me to do?

Prayerful Pause
Soften my resistance, O God, when I, like Jonah, am inclined to run the other way. Amen.

Meditation 22

Jonah 1:4-6

Perhaps Jonah, exhausted from his hurried trip to Joppa and worn out from some anxiety about this course of action he has taken, has gone down into the hold of the ship to sleep. But 'up top' a storm has begun to rage, caused by the Lord hurling "a great wind upon the sea."

The ship's officer comes to find him. "How can you be sleeping so deeply?" he asks with some exasperation. "Get up," he commands. "Call on your god! Perhaps the god will give some thought to us so that we won't perish."

The frightened ship's crew, made up of sailors from various locales, each with its designated god, call upon their gods and now turn to Jonah to bring his God into the mix. Might Jonah be re-thinking his impulsive act?

Sacred Ponderings
Anxiety can lead to some very ill-conceived decisions!

Prayerful Pause
"Slow me down, Lord, ease the pounding of my heart by the quieting of my mind."—from poem by Wilfred A. Peterson

Meditation 23

Jonah 1:7-10

Meanwhile, as Jonah is making his way up to join them, the sailors are casting lots to determine who brought this catastrophe upon them. This common method for making decisions, dividing property and gleaning insight from the gods, clearly demonstrates that the lot falls to Jonah. Perhaps his guilty conscience has gotten the better of him on this voyage because he has already shared with them before now that he is running from the Lord. They are full of questions for people in the midst of a raging storm! "Tell us since you are the cause of this evil happening to us: What do you do and where are you from? What's your country and and of what people are you?"

Jonah, who deluded himself into thinking he could run from God, now acknowledges God's presence in this storm and readily admits his identity: "I'm a Hebrew. I worship the Lord, the God of heaven—who made the sea and dry land." The sailors are now terrified! Jonah's God is over the sea and they know Jonah is on the run from his God. It is therefore an easy deduction that Jonah's God brought this storm about and something must be done to appease Jonah's God.

Sacred Ponderings
Have I ever "run from God"? Deluded myself about God?
Been terrified by God?

Prayerful Pause
When I am in rough waters, may my terror be mitigated by
God's Presence in the storm.

Meditation 24

Jonah 1:11-16

As the wind and the waters continues to rage, the crew seek the advice of Jonah for what is to be done to appease this God of his. Jonah, to his credit, doesn't try to avoid the consequences of his behavior. "Pick me up and hurl me into the sea!" he says, as he acknowledges this mess is his fault. "Then the sea will become calm around you." One imagines some of them were more than ready to toss him overboard. But even in the midst of this chaotic weather they attempt to spare him. They row for all they are worth in a futile attempt to reach dry land.

These men seem to be fast acquainting themselves with Jonah's God. They then pray, saying, "Please, Lord, don't let us perish on account of this man's life, and don't blame us for innocent blood! You are the Lord: whatever you want, you can do." And then they heave him over the side.

As Jonah had predicted, the sea ceases raging. These stunned and grateful sailors then worship the Lord "with a profound reverence." They offer sacrifices and we are told they make "solemn promises."

Sacred Ponderings
What "solemn promises" might these sailors have made?
What solemn promises have I made? Have I lived them out?

Prayerful Pause
May I live with a profound reverence for life and the Source of Life.
May that reverence mark all that I do. Amen.

Meditation 25

Jonah 1:17-2:10

Maybe in the now calm waters Jonah paddles around and contemplates his odds of survival. But before there is much time to consider that, the Lord provides "a great fish to swallow Jonah" and the fish's belly becomes Jonah's residence for three days and nights.

In this day and time, the sea was a mystery and a terrifying one at that, considered to be full of sea monsters. Being swallowed by a great fish would be one of the worst conceivable fates. Jonah, in his distress, cries out for help. Perhaps a psalm used in worship at the temple in Jerusalem takes form as a prayer of thanksgiving. From the depths of his soul he utters the words: "I called out to the Lord in my distress, and he answered me. From the belly of the underworld I cried out for help; you have heard my voice. You had cast me into the depths in the heart of the seas, and the flood surrounds me. All your strong waves and rushing water passed over me. So I said, 'I have been driven away from your sight. Will I ever again look on your holy temple?...I have sunk down to the underworld; its bars held me with no end in sight. But you brought me out of the pit...I will offer a sacrifice to you with a voice of thanks. That which I promised I will pay. Deliverance belongs to the Lord.'"

And then the Lord directs the fish to vomit Jonah onto dry land!

Sacred Ponderings
Once again we have reference to being brought "out of the pit." We think of Joseph placed in a pit by his brothers...Daniel in the pit of lions...Jonah in the pit of a great fish. What a common lot we share with people throughout the ages of finding ourselves in a pit...where we likely encounter God.

Prayerful Pause
May I recognize Your Presence in the pit, O God, and rely on Your grace and tender mercies towards me. Amen.

Meditation 26

Jonah 3:1-5

Before Jonah has even recovered from being spewed out of the belly of the great fish, the word of the Lord comes to him again, once again directing him to get up and go to Ninevah, to proclaim the message God has given him. This time Jonah doesn't hesitate. Off to Ninevah he goes, the image burnt into his memory of the belly of that "great fish." Not intending to disobey this time, no sir! Although archaeology has shown us that the wall around Nineveh was 7.5 miles, a large city for its time, it would not have been the three days that the story indicates it takes to cross it. The emphasis, though seems to intimate that Jonah is putting effort into this task he is now taking quite seriously.

As he is walking through the city he cries out "Just forty days more and Nineveh will be overthrown!" This is a man who has been in the depths because of ignoring God. His voice is punctuated with a sense of urgency, a resounding alarm for these people lest they ignore God too. And here is what scripture tells us happens: The people believe God. They proclaim a fast. They put on mourning clothes. And the writer makes a point that this is not just a handful of people who choose to take it seriously, but everyone "from the greatest of them to the least significant."

Sacred Ponderings
How seriously am I taking my relationship with God these days?

Prayerful Pause
O God, when I am tempted to dismiss You from my life,
help me instead to listen more closely. Amen

Meditation 27

Jonah 3:6-9

When the king of Assyria hears of this, he takes up the cry of repentance. However, one wonders about his understanding of repentance. He declares that all will fast, even the animals, and all will wear mourning clothes, even the animals. This seems less a demonstration of true repentance than it does a show of misguided power. The people have already begun to fast and are wearing mourning clothes. Insisting the animals fast and wear mourning clothes may be hyperbole to make a point but it comes off as so absurd as to make light of the seriousness of the situation.

However, he does indeed focus on the danger involved in failing to heed this warning. He declares they are all to call upon God forcefully. Their rituals of mourning often include wearing rough clothing such as goats' hair, tearing their clothing, putting dust or ashes on their heads. But reminiscent of the prophet Joel who urged the people of Judah to "tear their hearts and not their clothes" the people of Nineveh are commanded by the king to stop their evil behavior and violence. Out of these efforts he hopes "God may see this and turn from his wrath so that we might not perish."

Sacred Ponderings
What might it mean for me when confronted by my own transgressions, to "tear my heart?"

Prayer Pause
O Holy One, may I not trivialize or minimize my offenses but allow myself to see the consequences I have risked or allowed that disrupt my relationship with self, others and You, and to make amends as You direct me. Amen.

Meditation 28

Jonah 3:10-4:4

God sees that the people are repenting. The writer portrays a merciful and gracious God who honors their changes in heart and behavior and does not destroy them. Now one might expect that Jonah would be rejoicing. God had used him as a vessel to bring the people to repentance. They are now spared. He has played a significant role in this marvelous outcome. Instead "Jonah thought this was utterly wrong and was angry."

He complains bitterly to God. These people deserved punishment, he seems to be saying, and You didn't come through. He defends his fleeing God's command to him the first time as behavior that resulted from his certainty that God was going to forgive these degenerate people who didn't deserve such grace. One rendering of this might be: "They sure duped You, God. This little show of repentance hardly compensates for all their evil behavior. They are not now, nor were they ever, worthy of Your forgiveness."

Jonah gets quite dramatic. Much like the Hebrews wandering in the wilderness after leaving Egypt, he tells God to just "take my life from me, because it would be better for me to die than to live."

God, perhaps pondering whether he might point out a few inconsistencies in Jonah's life and logic, instead asks one simple and direct question: "Is your anger a good thing?"

Sacred Ponderings
Does any of this sound familiar? How many times do we judge others unworthy, for whatever reason, as though we have never done anything unworthy ourselves. Consider whether anger/judgement is ever called for and, if so, under what circumstances.

Prayerful Pause
Forgive my own short-sightedness and lack of understanding. May I grasp something of the enormity of Your compassion and recognize that I am as in need of it as anyone else. Amen.

Meditation 29

Jonah 4:5-8

Like a pouting four year old, Jonah goes out east of the city and makes a little canopy for himself where he sits and sulks. What he expects to come from this is hard to fathom. Does he think he will somehow sway God to punish them afterall? Or perhaps this is just for effect to make sure God knows just how angry he is?

But God is about to give Jonah a lesson about compassion. Seeing Jonah in the heat, he provides a shrub for better shade. Jonah is very pleased about this. Ah, we consider he might speculate, God now understands how upset he is and is now willing to "make up" after their "disagreement." But Jonah's pleasure is short-lived. The next day, God sends a worm to attack the shrub and as a consequence it dies. Then as the sun rises, God sends a dry east wind. The sun beats down on Jonah so that he becomes faint. In some additional melodrama he begs again to die: "It is better for me to die than to live."

His determination to influence God with his anger is only exceeded by his very shallow understanding of both God and the call he received from God in the first place.

Sacred Ponderings
What role does anger play in my life? How does it affect me internally? How does it impact my work, my relationships?

Prayerful Pause
Help me, O God, to see those times when anger can be used towards constructive ends as in countering injustice, and refuse to use it in ways that are harmful to others. Amen.

Meditation 30

Jonah 4:9-11

God again probes Jonah about his anger: "Is your anger about the shrub a good thing?" God asks. To what end is he angry? What purpose does he think it serves? One doubts Jonah even hesitates before responding: "Yes, my anger is good—even to the point of death!"

While Jonah's blood pressure rises and his sense of injured pride grows—didn't he proclaim the end of the Ninevites as instructed so they were at least forewarned before they were destroyed?—God drives home the point about compassion: "You pitied the shrub, for which you didn't work and which you didn't raise; it grew in a night and perished in a night. Yet for my part, can't I pity Nineveh, that great city, in which there are more than one hundred twenty thousand people who can't tell their right hand from their left, and also many animals?"

There is no resolution beyond this in our story of Jonah, no tidy ending where Jonah sees the error of his ways, gives thanks to God for healing his spiritual blindness. Thus we are left to deal with how this story may mirror our own spiritual blindness.

Sacred Ponderings

We might like to imagine Jonah as so removed from us. Surely we are better than this! But we usually don't have to dig very far beneath the surface of our own lives to recognize times when we hoped for some perceived enemy's downfall in some way.

Prayerful Pause

God I long to be Your person in the world, an ambassador for Your love. But I confess sometimes I have the heart of Jonah. I pray in times such as those that You will resurrect love in my heart and soul and mind. Amen.

Epilogue

Psalm 103:1-4

"Let my whole being bless the Lord! Let everything inside me bless his holy name! Let my whole being bless the Lord and never forget all his good deeds: how God forgives all your sins, heals all your sickness, saves your life from the pit, crowns you with faithful love and compassion."

We can surely recognize within ourselves those times we have been as faithful and trustworthy as Daniel as well as those times we have been as obstinate and obtuse as Jonah. The psalmist reminds us to always be grateful, to never forget God, who does indeed forgive us, heal us…and save us from the many pits into which we are prone to fall.

May these stories remind us of our own stories and of the ever faithful, ever generous, gracious, merciful Companion who travels with us on the journey.

Sacred Ponderings
Consider gratitude a daily spiritual practice.

Prayerful Pause
O God, may I be yearning always to grow in Your Spirit, seeking always to be a bearer of God's Dream-In-Progress. Amen.

www.ingramcontent.com/pod-product-compliance
Lightning Source LLC
Chambersburg PA
CBHW071007160426
43193CB00012B/1955